BESSER IN ENGLISCH

Weniger Fehler in Klassenarbeiten und Tests

9./10. Schuljahr

von Phyllis Driver
und Brian McCredie

Cornelsen
SCRIPTOR

Besser in Englisch, Weniger Fehler in Klassenarbeiten und Tests
– 9./10. Schuljahr –
wurde geplant und entwickelt von der Cornelsen & Oxford University Press GmbH, Berlin, im Auftrag des Cornelsen Verlags Scriptor, Berlin.

Verfasser Phyllis Driver, München
Brian McCredie, München

Gedruckt auf chlorfrei gebleichtem Papier ohne Dioxinbelastung der Gewässer

Die Deutsche Bibliothek – CIP-Einheitsaufnahme

Besser in Englisch – Berlin: Cornelsen Scriptor
(Lernhilfen von Cornelsen Scriptor)
Weniger Fehler in Klassenarbeiten und Tests: 9./10. Schuljahr
von Phyllis Driver und Brian McCredie. – 1997
ISBN 3-589-21073-7

1. Auflage ✔
6. 5. 4. 3. 2. Die letzten Ziffern bezeichnen
2002 01 00 99 98 Zahl und Jahr des Druckes.

Redaktion Helga Holtkamp unter Mitarbeit von Barbara Swayne, Annabel Haslam und Vera Olbricht

Layout Britta Dieterle, Berlin

Umschlaggestaltung Studio Lochmann, Frankfurt am Main,
unter Verwendung eines Fotos von Michael Seifert, Hannover

Druck & Weiterverarbeitung Freiburger Graphische Betriebe, Freiburg

Printed in Germany
ISBN 3-589-21073-7
Bestellnummer 210737

Inhalt

Vorwort

Möchtest du besser in englischen Klassenarbeiten und Tests abschneiden?

Dieses Buch richtet sich an alle, die kleinere oder größere Probleme im Fach Englisch in der Sekundarstufe 1 haben. Es zeigt dir Wege auf, wie du deine Fehler in Klassenarbeiten und Tests wesentlich reduzieren kannst.

- **Besser in Englisch: Weniger Fehler in Klassenarbeiten und Tests** ist lehrwerkunabhängig und für die Klassen 9 und 10 an Real- und Gesamtschulen und Gymnasien gedacht. Es eignet sich besonders gut zum Selbststudium.

- Der Stoff orientiert sich an den wesentlichen grammatischen Strukturen der gesamten Sekundarstufe 1 und nimmt die häufigsten Fehlerquellen unter die Lupe.

- Der Wortschatz entspricht in etwa dem, der bis zum Ende der Klasse 9 vermittelt wird. Da die unterschiedlichen Lehrwerke im Wortschatz nicht immer übereinstimmen, kann es sein, dass du das eine oder andere Wort nachschlagen musst. Ein zweisprachiges Wörterbuch, das für die gesamte Sekundarstufe 1 besonders geeignet ist, ist **Das Oxford Schulwörterbuch,** ***English–German, Deutsch–Englisch;*** Bestellnummer 27554 (kart.) und 27422 (geb.).

- Im Inhaltsverzeichnis kannst du die Punkte heraussuchen, die dir besondere Schwierigkeiten bereiten. Die einzelnen Abschnitte in den Teilen A und B kannst du in beliebiger Reihenfolge durcharbeiten. An den Teil C solltest du dich erst machen, wenn du A und B durchgearbeitet hast.

- Im Teil A (Seite 7 – 38) werden die sprachlichen Fehler intensiv behandelt, die entstehen, wenn man zu sehr auf Deutsch denkt und aus der eigenen Sprache direkt ins Englische übersetzt. So enstehen Fehler im Bereich Wortverwechslungen (*technology* – Technik), Rechtschreibung (*address* – Adresse), Falsche Freunde (*action* – Aktion) oder Singular und Plural (*damage* – Schäden).

- Im **Teil B** (Seite 39 – 100) werden die wichtigsten grammatischen Strukturen kurz erläutert und anschließend geübt, wie z.B. die unterschiedlichen Zeiten und ihre Verwendung, Adjektive und Adverben und ihre Steigerung oder die Wortstellung. In diesem Teil werden außerdem die wichtigsten Kommaregeln erklärt, was bei einer Klassenarbeit durchaus von Bedeutung sein kann.

- Im **Teil C** (Seite 101 – 115) kann man zum Schluss seine Kenntnisse in mehreren Tests überprüfen.

- Jedes Kapitel in den Teilen A und B fängt mit einem Multiple Choice Test an, den du aus dem Stehgreif lösen solltest, ohne die Grammatikerläuterungen zu lesen. Hier kannst du sehen, wie viel du tatsächlich schon weißt und wo deine Schwächen liegen.

- Danach solltest du die Erklärungen durcharbeiten und die anschließenden Übungen machen.

- Eine Fülle von nützlichen **Exam Tips** wird die helfen, besonders häufige Fehler ein für allemal zu vermeiden.

- Die Lösungen (Seite 116 – 120) sind nicht nur zur Selbstkontrolle da, sondern auch als Hilfe gedacht, falls du einmal gar nicht weiterkommst. Du solltest aber immer daran denken, dass bloßes Abschreiben herzlich wenig bringt.

- Im übrigen ist dieses Werk sowohl eine Ergänzung zu **Besser in Englisch: Grammatik 9./10. Schuljahr** (Bestellnummer 209 038) als auch ein Einstieg in **Besser in Englisch: Weniger Fehler in Klausuren, Oberstufe** (Bestellnummer 210 745).

Und nun wünschen dir die Autoren viel Spaß, viel Erfolg und vor allem viel bessere Noten!

Phyllis Driver
Brian McLeod

Bildnachweis

Seite 9:	IFA-BILDERTEAM, Düsseldorf
Seite 17:	IFA-BILDERTEAM, Düsseldorf
Seite 19:	The Stock Market, Düsseldorf
Seite 31:	BAVARIA Bildagentur, Düsseldorf
Seite 35:	Duncan Smith, London
Seite 49:	IMAGE BANK, Berlin
Seite 59:	The Stock Market, Düsseldorf
Seite 77:	Archiv für Kunst und Geschichte, Berlin
Seite 82:	IFA-BILDERTEAM, Düsseldorf
Seite 89:	IMAGE BANK, Berlin
Seite 93:	IFA-BILDERTEAM, Düsseldorf
Seite 94:	IFA-BILDERTEAM, Düsseldorf
Seite 100:	Archiv für Kunst und Geschichte, Berlin
Seite 108:	Plimoth Plantation, Inc.
Seite 111 :	Helga Lade Fotoagentur, Berlin
Seite 114:	IMAGE BANK, Berlin

Alle Zeichnungen (außer S. 35) von Christine Georg, Dortmund.

Hinweise zu verwendeten Abkürzungen und Symbolen:

BE	bedeutet Britisches Englisch
AE	bedeutet Amerikanisches Englisch

~ Dieses Symbol wird dir öfter begegnen.
Es weist auf Wörter hin, die du einsetzen sollst.

A

Hi, I'm Nicky and this is my friend Oliver.
Hallo, ich heiße Oliver. Mit Nicky spreche ich meistens Englisch.

A 1 Singular oder Plural?

Streiche jeden Satz, in dem du einen Fehler findest.

1.1 His knowledges of English must be good.
1.2 His knowledge of English must be good.
1.3 His English knowledges must be good.

2.1 She earned one thousand dollar in two month.
2.2 She earned one thousand dollars in two month.
2.3 She earned one thousand dollars in two months.

3.1 No progress has been made.
3.2 No progresses has been made.
3.3 No progress have been made.

4.1 Please explain it me.
4.2 Please explain it to me.

5.1 What means this word?
5.2 What does this word mean?
5.3 What mean this word?

6.1 The good news has surprised me.
6.2 A good news has surprised me.
6.3 The good news have surprised me.

7.1 Nowadays the most people don't go to church.
7.2 Nowadays most of the people don't go to church.
7.3 Nowadays most people don't go to church.
7.4 Nowadays the most of the people don't go to church.

8.1 We gave her a good advice.
8.2 We gave her good advice.
8.3 We gave her good advices.

9.1 Marc is working as photographer.
9.2 Marc is working as a photographer.
9.3 Marc is working as a photograph.
9.4 Marc is working as photography.

Hast du das gekonnt?
Falls du nicht alle falschen Sätze identifiziert hast, mache weiter mit diesem Abschnitt (Seite 9).
Falls du die Aufgabe richtig lösen konntest, kannst du mit dem nächsten Abschnitt (Seite 11) weitermachen.

➤ Recht viele Fehler in Klausuren haben wenig mit sprachlichen Regeln zu tun. Sie entstehen, weil man auf Deutsch denkt und die Besonderheiten des Englischen übersieht bzw. vergessen hat.

Um nur ein Beispiel zu nennen: Wenn man im Deutschen eine Pluralform benutzt, kann es sein, dass man im Englischen einen Singular braucht, z.B. *Schäden* – damage.
Das Wort damages dagegen bedeutet Schadensersatz!

Was man also direkt aus der einen Sprache übernimmt, ist häufig falsch in der anderen.

➤ Substantiv und Verb im Singular

advice - *Ratschläge* (a piece of, word of, bit of / some advice - *ein Ratschlag)*
damage - *Schäden*
furniture - *Möbel* (a piece of furniture - *ein Möbelstück)*
hair - *Haare*
information - *Informationen* (a piece of / bit of / some information - *eine Information)*
knowledge - *Kenntnisse* (knowledge of - ... *Kenntnisse)*
news - *Nachrichten* (a piece of / bit of / some news - *eine Nachricht)*
progress - *Fortschritte*
proof - *Beweise*

➤ Substantiv und Verb im Plural

binoculars - *Fernglas*
contents - *Inhalt*
goods - *(Handels-)Ware*
outskirts - *Außen-, Randgebiet*
surroundings - *Umgebung*

➤ Substantiv im Plural, Verb im Singular

darts - *Darts, Würfelspiel*
the Netherlands - *die Niederlande*
politics - *Politik*
the United Nations (UN) - *die Vereinten Nationen*
the United States (USA) - *die Vereinigten Staaten*

Exam Tip 1 Denk daran, niemals Sätze in der Art zu schreiben, wie ~~*Speaks he English?*~~ oder ~~*Explained you it to him?*~~ Hier ist eine Form des Hilfsverbs ***do*** erforderlich: ***Does*** *he* ***speak*** *English? /* ***Did*** *you* ***explain*** *it to him?*

Exam Tip 2 Übrigens heißt es ***explain / give / hand out / say …*** *something* ***to*** *someone!*

Exam Tip 3 Im Englischen gibt es endlos viele Besonderheiten wie
arbeiten als Fotografin – *work as* ***a*** *photographer*
die meisten Leute – *most people*
$20 – *twenty* ***dollars***
DM 5 – *five* ***marks***
zwei Monate – *two* ***months:*** Hier vergisst man leicht das ***s***, weil das Wort schwer auszusprechen ist.

Exercise 1 Übersetze die farbigen Wörter und setze die richtige Verbform ein.

1 *Viele Schäden sind gemacht worden.*

A lot of ______________________________ been done.

has / have

2 *Mein Fernglas liegt auf dem Rucksack.*

______________________________ on the rucksack.

is lying / are lying

3 *Seine Französischkenntnisse waren ausgezeichnet.*

______________________________ excellent.

was / were

4 *Ein guter Ratschlag hilft im richtigen Moment.*

______________________________ at the right moment.

helps / help

5 *Deine guten Ratschläge waren recht nützlich.* ______________

______________________________ very useful. was / were

6 *Guten Abend! Sie hören die Nachrichten.* Good evening!

Here ______________________________ . is / are

7 *Schon damals glaubte ich, dass die Beweise nicht besonders überzeugend waren.* Even then I believed that ______________ ______________ especially convincing. wasn't / weren't

8 *Er musste es ihr mehrmals erklären.* He had to ______________ ______________ several times.

9 *Wie übersetzte sie dieses Wort?* How ______________ ______________ this word?

10 *Die Vereinigten Staaten besitzen viele Waffen.* ______________ lots of weapons. possesses / possess

11 *Die meisten Leute genießen einen Strandurlaub.* ______________ ______________ a holiday on the beach. enjoy / enjoys

12 *Die Ware wiegt zweihundert Kilo.* ______________ . weighs / weigh

13 *Versteht er dich? Oder spricht er kein Englisch?* ______________ you? Or ______________ any English?

14 *Politik ist ein hartes Geschäft.* ______________ a hard business. is / are

15 *Ich möchte nicht als Krankenschwester arbeiten.* I wouldn't like to work ______________ .

16 *Einige neue Informationen sind gerade eingetroffen.* ______________ ______________ just arrived. has / have

Exercise 2 Übersetze nun den ganzen Satz.

1 *Gute Möbel sind oft recht teuer.*

____

2 *Die Umgebung ist nicht besonders schön hier.*

____

3 *Erklär' mir die Geschichte nochmals, bitte.*

____

4 *Keine Nachrichten sind gute Nachrichten.*

____

5 *Zwei Pfund Äpfel kosten vier Mark.*

____

6 *Seine Haare waren lang und blond.*

____

Exam Tip 4 Niemals ein Komma im Englischen vor ***that*** im Sinne von **dass** (vgl. Satz 7 in *Exercise 1).*

Exam Tip 5 Vorsicht bei dem Wort **schon**, denn ***already*** ist als Übersetzung oft fehl am Platz. Entweder gibt es kein richtiges Äquivalent
Wir warten **schon** zwei Stunden. – *We've been waiting two hours.*
oder es wird z.B. so übersetzt:
Schon damals ... – ***Even*** *then* ... (vgl. Satz 7 in *Exercise 1);*
Schon als er ankam ... – ***As soon as*** *he arrived ... ;*
Schon um vier Uhr morgens ... – ***As early as*** *four o'clock in the morning ...*

A 2 Wörter, die man leicht verwechselt

Streiche jeden Satz, in dem du einen Fehler findest.

1.1 She said that she didn't want to come.
1.2 She told that she didn't want to come.
1.3 She said me that she didn't want to come.

2.1 She attended a high school for five years.
2.2 She visited a high school for five years.

3.1 In the last century millions left Europe to immigrate to the USA.
3.2 In the last century millions left Europe to emigrate to the USA.

4.1 Wages have raised 5% this year.
4.2 Wages have risen 5% this year.
4.3 They have risen wages 5% this year.

5.1 He won first price.
5.2 The prize of petrol has fallen.
5.3 Everyone has heard of the Nobel Prize.

6.1 Some peoples at the meeting protested.
6.2 Some people at the meeting protested.

7.1 I made lots of photos on holiday.
7.2 I did lots of photos on holiday.
7.3 I took lots of photos on holiday.

8.1 Please control these figures again.
8.2 Have you controlled his passport?
8.3 You must control your feelings.

9.1 Have you already made the housework?
9.2 Have you already done the housework?

10.1 What will the firm's new policy be?
10.2 What will the firm's new politics be?

11.1 That problem won't effect us.
11.2 The affect could be serious.
11.3 Did the illness affect you?

Hast du das gekonnt?
Falls du nicht alle falschen Sätze identifizieren konntest, mache weiter mit diesem Abschnitt (Seite 14).
Ansonsten kannst du mit dem nächsten Abschnitt anfangen (Seite 20).

➤ Wortverwechslungen passieren leicht im Englischen, oft bei fast identischen Vokabeln wie: **people** – *Leute* ≠ **peoples** – *Völker.*

Manchmal ähneln sich zwei Wörter in Aussprache und Schreibweise: to **emigrate** – *auswandern* ≠ to **immigrate** – *einwandern,* **price** – *(Kauf)Preis* ≠ **prize** – *(Sieges)Preis.*

Oder vielleicht hat das Deutsche nur einen Begriff für zwei verschiedene Begriffe im Englischen: **policy** – *Politik oder Linie (einer Firma, Regierung, …)* ≠ **politics** – *(Partei)Politik.*

Am besten man merkt sich die **Zusammenhänge** – sonst ist ein Fehler so sicher wie eine Sechs in der nächsten Klassenarbeit!

➤ Verwechslungen beim Verb

affect – *betreffen* ≠ **effect** – *bewirken, (Aus)Wirkung*
appreciate – *zu schätzen wissen* ≠ **estimate** – *(ab-, ein)schätzen*
attend – *besuchen (Schule, Uni)* ≠
  visit – *besuchen (Freund, Stadt)*
become – *werden* ≠ **get** – *bekommen*
borrow – *von jmdm. etwas borgen* ≠
  lend – *an jmdn. etwas verleihen*
bring – *(her)bringen (zum Sprecher)* ≠
  take – *(hin-, weg)bringen (vom Sprecher)*
check – *(über)prüfen, kontrollieren* ≠ **control** – *beherrschen*
lay [laid, has laid] – *legen* ≠ **lie** [lay, lain] – *liegen*
raise – *(an)heben; erhöhen (Gehalt)* ≠ **rise** – *(auf)steigen*
remember – *sich erinnern (an)* ≠
  remind someone (of) sth. – *jmdn. an etwas erinnern*
say (sth. to someone) – *sagen* ≠ **tell** (someone sth.) – *sagen, erzählen*

➤ Wie übersetzt man „machen“?

eine Prüfung machen – to **take** / **do** / **sit** an exam
ein Foto machen – to **take** a photo
eine Erfahrung machen – to **have** an experience
seine Hausaufgabe(n) machen – to **do** one's homework
die Haus(halts)arbeit machen – to **do** the housework
einen Fehler machen – to **make** a mistake
Fortschritte machen – to **make** progress

Und übrigens: *Tee kochen* – to **make** tea

···· Exam Tip 6 Nach *tell* kein *that*-Satz in der Art: ~~*He told that he had seen it*~~.

Exercise 1 Übersetze die farbigen Satzteile.

1 *Er erinnert mich an meinen Vater.*

________________________________ my father.

2 *Erinnerst du dich an den alten Witz?*

________________________________ that old joke?

3 *Er legte seine Karten auf den Tisch.*

____________________ his cards on the table.

4 *Wir mussten das Geld von der Bank leihen.*

We had to ________________________________ .

5 *Kannst du mir deine Oasis CD leihen?*

________________________________ ?

6 *Die Regierung will den Lebensstandard anheben.*

The government wants to ____________ the standard of living.

7 *Der Lebensstandard stieg im letzten Jahr.*

________________________________ last year.

8 *Bis morgen werde ich eine Antwort bekommen.*

By tomorrow __________________________ an answer.

9 *Wir schätzen Ihre Hilfe sehr.*

__________________________ your help very much.

10 *Ich schätze den Preis auf $25.*

____________________________ to be $25.

11 *Können Sie dem Chef diese Briefe bringen?*

__________________________ these letters to the boss?

12 *Überprüfen Sie die Ergebnisse nochmals.*

____________________________ the results again.

13 *Es hat schon Wochen lang da gelegen.*

____________________________ there for weeks.

Exercise 2 Setze das passende Verb ein. (Die Verbform braucht man nicht zu ändern.) ~ **take**; **do**; **have**; **make**

1 Could you __________ some more tea, please?

2 You __________ mistakes the whole time.

3 I have to __________ the exam in June.

4 I wouldn't like to __________ an experience like that.

5 We usually __________ lots of photos on holiday.

➤ Verwechslungen beim Substantiv

chips – *Pommes frites* ≠ **crisps** – *Chips*
employee – *Arbeitnehmer/in* ≠ **employer** – *Arbeitgeber/in*
man – *Mann* ≠ **husband** – *(Ehe)Mann*
permission – *Erlaubnis* ≠ **permit** – *Genehmigung(sschein)*
road – *(Land)Straße* ≠ **street** – *Straße (in einer Ortschaft)*
technique – *Verfahren, Technik, Methode* ≠
technology – *Technologie, Technik*
wife – *(Ehe)Frau* ≠ **woman** – *Frau*

➤ Verwechslungen beim Adjektiv

big – *groß (Wagen, Stadt)* ≠ **great** – *großartig, toll (Idee, Urlaub), bedeutend, beträchtlich (Unterschied, Zahl)*
economic – *(volks)wirtschaftlich, Wirtschafts-* ≠ **economical** – *sparsam*
fat – *dick (Mensch, Profit)* ≠
thick – *dick (Buch, Mauer), dicht (Haare, Wald), doof*
hard – *schwer (Leben, Zeiten)* ≠ **heavy** – *schwer (Gewicht, Last)* ≠
serious – *schwer (Krankheit, Krise, Problem)*

Exercise 3 Setze jeweils die passende Entsprechung für das deutsche Wort ein.

1 Japan is at the centre of modern ________________ . ↝ *Technik*

2 Every artist has a different ________________ . ↝ *Technik*

3 A ______________ crisis has developed. ↝ *schwer*

4 Most kids ask their parents for ____________________ to stay out late. ↝ *Erlaubnis*

5 You'll need a ____________________ from the customs officer. ↝ *Genehmigung[sschein]*

6 I don't want ________________ , I will buy __________________ and a hamburger. ↝ *Chips; Pommes frites*

7 After Exeter take the ________________ to Plymouth – we live in Tregantle ________________ in Plymouth. ↝ *Straße; Straße*

8 It really is __________________ to make a ________________ profit at last! ↝ *großartig; dick*

9 The __________________ situation in Britain is improving. ↝ *Wirtschafts-*

10 Scots people are supposed to be very _________________ . ↝ *sparsam*

11 My _______________ and I first met four years ago. ↝ *Mann*

12 There are often all sorts of problems between an ____________________ and an ____________________ . ↝ *Arbeitnehmer; Arbeitgeber*

13 Ask my ______________ – she'll know. ↝ *Frau*

➤ Andere Verwechslungen

as – *wie*
typische Verbindungen:
as **soon**, **quickly**, … as
(not) as **young**, **big**, … as

like – *wie*
typische Verbindungen:
to **talk**, **behave**, … like
like **me**, **him**, **them**, …
a **person**, **woman**, … like

few – *wenige* ≠ **a few** – *ein paar, einige (wenige)*
first – *(zu)erst, zunächst* ≠ **at first** – *anfangs* ≠ **firstly** – *erstens*
neither (of) – *keine(r) (von zweien)* ≠
none (of) – *keine(r) (von mehreren)*
of – *von* ≠ **off** – *von … herunter*

Exam Tip 7 Das Verb ***to lose*** schreibt sich immer nur mit **einem *o***.
Nicht verwechseln mit ***loose*** – locker!

Exam Tip 8 Im Deutschen ist es möglich **eine Erlaubnis** zu sagen.
Im Englischen dagegen benutzt man ***permission*** **ohne *a*!**

Exercise 4 Übersetze die farbigen Satzteile mit einer passenden Entsprechung aus den Erklärungen bzw. den Examtips.

1 *Ich mache es so bald wie möglich und so sorgfältig wie möglich*

I'll do it ______________________ and

______________________ .

2 *Er ist genau wie ich, in jeder Hinsicht.*

______________________ in every way.

3 *Arbeiter wie wir haben keine Zukunft.*

______________________ have no future.

4 *Willst du alle vier Zeitschriften kaufen? – Nein, keine der vier.*

Do you want to buy all four magazines? –

________________________________ .

5 *Hast du beide Romane gelesen? – Nein, keinen.*

Have you read both novels? – ________________________ .

6 *Erstens will ich erzählen, was ich zuerst gemacht habe.*

____________ I want to say what I did ____________ .

7 *Anfangs hatte ich wenige Freunde in der Gruppe. Nur ein paar von den Mädchen mochten mich.*

______________ I had __________________ in the group.

Only __________________________________ liked me.

8 *Verlieren Sie Ihren Reisepass nicht! Sie haben ihn schon einmal verloren.*

Don't _______________ your passport! You've ______________ it once already.

Exam Tip 9 Das Verb **bekommen** in dem Ausdruck **ein Kind bekommen** heißt auf Englisch ***to have a child***. Niemals ~~to get a child~~.

Exam Tip 10 Das Verb **starten** im Zusammenhang mit Flugzeugen heißt entweder ***to take off*** oder ***to depart***. Niemals ~~to start~~ – anfangen!

A 3 Falsche Freunde

Unterstreiche in jeder Gruppe den Satz bzw. die Sätze, in denen das Englisch nicht misslungen ist.

1.1 My note in French was really low.
1.2 I left a note for you on your desk.
1.3 These are the best notes I've ever had.
1.4 These two notes are worth 100.

2.1 Seven hundred pupils study at our gymnasium.
2.3 Annie is learning Latin at the gymnasium.
2.3 Judy does karate at the gymnasium twice a week.

3.1 Cecil Beaton was a famous British photography.
3.2 Cecil Beaton was a famous British photograph.
3.3 Cecil Beaton was a famous British photo.
3.4 Cecil Beaton was a famous British photographer.

4.1 You can become your visa over there.
4.2 You can get your visa over there.
4.3 I'll become more if I get a better job.

5.1 We stayed the night in a Cornish pension.
5.2 Your pension depends on your income.
5.3 Can you recommend a cheap pension in the town?
5.4 All our workers receive pensions.

6.1 Jack the Ripper committed six murderers.
6.2 He's probably the world's best-known murder.
6.3 They never discovered the murderer's identity.
6.4 To murder his victims *[Opfer]* he used a knife.

7.1 He blames himself for the accident.
7.2 He's blamed himself again, in front of everybody, with his stupid behaviour.
7.3 He only has himself to blame for what's happened.

8.1 What time does the film start?
8.2 What time does the plane start?
8.3 What time does the play start?
8.4 The aircraft crashed just after the start.

Hast du das gekonnt?
Falls du nicht alle falschen Sätze identifiziert hast, mache weiter mit diesem Abschnitt (Seite 21).
Falls du die Aufgabe richtig lösen konntest, kannst du zum nächsten Abschnitt (Seite 24) gehen.

➤ Es gibt das eine oder andere Wort im Deutschen, dessen Schreibweise vermuten lässt, dass es genau die gleiche Bedeutung hat wie eine Entsprechung im Englischen (z.B. **brav** von brave – *tapfer*). Forget it! Solche Vokabeln nennt man, aus gutem Grunde, false friends.

➤ **Diese Vokabeln sollte man nicht verwechseln!**

Aktion – **campaign** ≠ **action** – *Handlung, Tat*
aktuell – **current** (fashion, problem, ...) ≠ **actual** (Adj.) – *eigentlich,*
actually (Adv.) – *wirklich, tatsächlich*
Allee – **avenue** ≠ **alley** – *(schmale) Gasse*
also – **so**, **therefore** ≠ **also** – *auch*

bekommen – **get** ≠ **become** – *werden*
sich blamieren – to **make** a fool of oneself ≠
to **blame** someone – *jmdm. die Schuld geben*
brav – **good**, **well** behaved ≠ **brave** – *tapfer, mutig*

Chef/in – **boss** ≠ **chef** – *Küchenchef/in, Chefkoch/köchin*
Christ – **Christian** ≠ **Christ** – *Christus*

Fotograf/in – **photographer** ≠ **photograph** – *Fotografie, Bild*

Gymnasium – **grammar school** ≠ **gymnasium** – *Turnhalle*

Hochschule – **university**, **college** ≠ **high school** (AE) – *Oberschule (USA)*

konsequent – **consistent** ≠ **consequently** – *folglich, daher*

Labor – **lab(oratory)** ≠ **labor** (AE), **labour** (BE) – *Arbeit(s-)*

Marmelade – **jam** ≠ **marmalade** – *Orangenmarmelade*
Meinung – **opinion** ≠ **meaning** – *Bedeutung*
Mörder – **murderer** ≠ **murder**, to **murder** – *Mord, ermorden*

Note – **mark** (BE), **grade** (AE) ≠
note, to **note** (BE) – *(Geld)Schein, Notiz, notieren*

Pension – **guest house**, **boarding house** ≠
pension – *Altersrente, Pension*

sensibel – **sensitive** ≠ **sensible** – *vernünftig*
Start – **take-off** ≠ **start**, to **start** – *Anfang, anfangen*
starten – to **take off**
sympathisch – **lik(e)able** ≠ **sympathetic** – *mitfühlend*

Exercise 1 Übersetze die farbigen Satzteile mit einer passenden Entsprechung aus den Erklärungen.

1 *Was ist deine Meinung über die königliche Familie?*

What's ______________________________ of the Royal Family?

2 *Diese Bedeutung des Wortes ist ungewöhnlich.*

______________________________ of the word is unusual.

3 *Unser Gymnasium besitzt eine sehr moderne Turnhalle.*

______________________ has ______________________________ .

4 *Das ist gewiss eine vernünftige Idee.*

That's certainly ______________________________ .

5 Eigentlich glaube ich, dass AIDS das schlimmste von allen aktuellen Problemen ist.

__________________ I think that AIDS is the worst of all ______________ problems.

6 *Die tatsächliche Gefahr war nicht sehr groß.*

______________________________ wasn't very big.

7 *Er wird eine Stelle an einer Hochschule bekommen.*

He'll ______________ a position at a ______________________________ .

8 *Sie unterrichtet an einer Oberschule in den USA.*

She teaches at ______________________________ in the USA.

9 *Marc ist ein braver, sehr sensibler Junge.*

Marc is ______________________________ .

10 *Es wäre interessant, in einem Labor zu arbeiten.*

It would be interesting ______________________________ .

11 *Jutta kaufte eine kleine Pension mit einem Teil von ihrer Altersrente.*

Jutta bought ______________________________ with a part of her ____________________ .

12 *Tapfer ist er ja, aber nicht gerade sympathisch.*

He's ____________ all right, but not exactly __________________ .

13 *Sei konsequent in dem, was du machst.*

Be __________________ in what you do.

14 *Nicht schon wieder Orangenmarmelade!*

Ich mag nur Erdbeermarmelade.

Not ________________ again!

But I only like strawberry ________ .

15 *Paris ist eine Mischung aus alten*

Gassen und eleganten Alleen.

Paris is a mixture of _____________

__________________________ .

Exercise 2 Richtig oder falsch? Bessere die falschen Sätze entsprechend aus.

1 Every Christian believes in Christus.
2 The current advertising action will be expensive.
3 Who's the chef of this company?
4 She acted consequently, and that's why she's been successful.
5 The labor market in the USA is in a difficult situation.
6 We design PCs in our labor.
7 After my father died, everyone was very sympathetic towards me.
8 He can cook better than any of the chefs at the Ritz in London.
9 She's always dressed in the actual fashion.
10 The murder went to prison for murder.

···· Exam Tip 11 Das Wort ***police*** wird immer wie ein **Plural** behandelt, d.h. **Die Polizei ist** da. – ***The police are*** *here.*

···· Exam Tip 12 Um **sicher(lich)** zu übersetzen, benutzt man am besten ***certain(ly)*** und nicht ***sure(ly)***. Warum? Weil ***sure(ly)*** meistens ausdrückt, dass etwas nicht sicher ist:
Er wird **sicherlich** kommen. – *He'll* ***certainly*** *come.*
Aber: ***Surely,*** *he'll come, won't he?* – Er wird **wohl noch** / **hoffentlich** kommen, oder?

A 4 Gleiche Aussprache – unterschiedliche Schreibweise

Streiche jeden Satz, in dem du einen Fehler findest.

1.1 I think there's something wrong with the breaks.
1.2 He breaks all the time when he's driving.
1.3 Have the brakes been repaired?
1.4 The vase might brake if you're not careful.

2.1 The rode ends near Lower Tregantle.
2.2 We road all the way along the beach.
2.3 Is this the road we rode along to Polperro?

3.1 Production has grown in the passed years.
3.2 Production has grown in the past years.
3.3 Production has grown in the passed.

4.1 I've gone threw the whole book now.
4.2 I've gone through the hole book now.
4.3 I've gone through the whole book now.

5.1 I red your letter just last week.
5.2 I read your letter just last week.
5.3 I read your letter just last weak.

6.1 It didn't cost a single cent.
6.2 It didn't cost a single sent.

7.1 Their our new neighbours over they're.
7.2 There our new neighbours over there.
7.3 They're our new neighbours over their.
7.4 They're our new neighbours over there.

8.1 Its time for me to leave.
8.2 It's time for me to leave.

9.1 Have you heard wether the weather will improve?
9.2 Have you heard whether the weather will improve?
9.3 Have you heard whether the wheather will improve?

10.1 The steal industry is in a crisis.
10.2 The steel industry is in a crisis.

Hast du das gekonnt?
Falls du nicht alle falschen Sätze identifiziert hast, mache weiter mit diesem Abschnitt (Seite 25).
Ansonsten mache weiter mit dem nächsten Abschnitt (Seite 26).

➤ Es gibt auch **false friends** von einer anderen Sorte, und zwar die – nicht wenigen – englischen Wörter, die so klingen, als ob sie etwas miteinander zu tun hätten: Identische Aussprache, ähnliche Schreibweise, jedoch eine **andere** Bedeutung!

blew (to blow) – *blasen* ≠ **blue** – *blau*
passed (to pass) – *vorbeigehen* ≠ **past** – *Vergangenheit; vergangen*
board – *Tafel; Brett* ≠ **bored** – *gelangweilt*
peace – *Friede* ≠ **piece** – *Stück*
brake (to brake) – *Bremse; bremsen* ≠ **break** (to **break**) – *Pause; brechen*
read (to read) – *lesen* ≠ **red** – *rot*
Britain – *Großbritannien* ≠ **Briton** – *Brite, Britin*
road – *(Land)Straße* ≠ **rode** (to ride) – *geritten; reiten*
cent – *Cent (US-Münze)* ≠ **sent** (to send) – *schicken* ≠ **scent** – *Duft*
steal – *stehlen* ≠ **steel** – *Stahl*
there – *da(hin), dort(hin)* ≠ **their** – *ihr(e)* ≠
they're [*Kurzform von* they are]
dear – *lieb* ≠ **deer** – *Reh*
fair – *gerecht; Messe* ≠ **fare** – *Fahrpreis*
threw (to throw) – *werfen* ≠ **through** – *durch*
heard (to hear) – *hören* ≠ **herd** – *Herde*
weak – *schwach* ≠ **week** – *Woche*
hole – *Loch* ≠ **whole** – *ganz*
weather – Wetter ≠ **whether** – *ob*
it's [*Kurzform von* it is / has] ≠ **its** – *sein(e); ihr(e)*
which – *welcher, der, was* ≠ **witch** – *Hexe*

Exercise Richtig oder falsch? Bessere jeden falschen Satz entsprechend aus.

1 He began the letter with “Deer Sir or Madam”.
2 Its not fare to expect people to pay such a high price for a ticket to the fare next week.
3 Great Briton’s whole economy depends very much on it’s oil production.
4 I herd or read somewhere that red is a colour witch, in China, is supposed to bring good luck.
5 Their’s only one peace of cake left, I’m afraid.
6 They’re are heards of dear all over Scotland. We saw lots of them when we drove threw the Highlands.

A 5 Rechtschreibung mit Tücken

Streiche jeden Satz, in dem du einen Fehler findest.

1.1 I'll send a telegramm to his Berlin appartment.
1.2 I'll send a telegram to his Berlin appartment.
1.3 I'll send a telegram to his Berlin apartment.

2.1 The goverment must do more for the enviroment.
2.2 The government must do more for the enviromnent.
2.3 The governmnent must do more for the environment.
2.4 The government must do more for the environment.

3.1 There's an adress on the cassette.
3.2 There's an address on the casette.
3.3 There's an address on the cassette.

4.1 The disaster happened on the eighth day of the twelvth month.
4.2 The disaster happened on the eightht day of the twelfth month.
4.3 The disaster happened on the eighth day of the twelfth month.

5.1 Most germans know a few english words.
5.2 Most Germans know a few english words.
5.3 Most Germans know a few English words.

6.1 The lack *[Mangel]* of succes is disappointing.
6.2 The lack of sucess is disappointing.
6.3 The lack of success is dissappointing.
6.4 The lack of success is disappointing.

7.1 Your help won't be neccesary.
7.2 Your help won't be necessary.

Hast du das gekonnt?
Auch wenn du die Aufgabe vollständig richtig lösen konntest,
mache trotzdem weiter mit diesem Abschnitt –
er ist besonders wichtig!

Exam Tip 13 Ob ein Wort mit oder ohne Bindestrich geschrieben wird, verwirrt auch die meisten Angelsachsen, denn die Schreibweise ist auch in verschiedenen Wörterbüchern uneinheitlich.
Der moderne Trend geht allmählich (auf beiden Seiten des Atlantiks) dahin, zwei Wörter ohne Bindestrich zu schreiben:
z.B. *felt tip* – Filzstift, *dining room, sailing ship* – etc.

Es gibt übrigens im Englischen fast nie einen Bindestrich bei Abkürzung plus Substantiv:
UN-Truppen – *UN troops;* **NATO-Konferenz** – *NATO conference;* ...
Aber: *A-Level (BE)* – etwa: Abitur.
Richte dich nach dem im Unterricht gebrauchten Lehrwerk!

➤ Dass man ein Wort richtig schreiben kann, spielt eine wesentliche Rolle bei jeder Klassenarbeit. Einige klare Richtlinien sind hier sicherlich von Nutzen, auch wenn es auf diesem Gebiet leider von Ausnahmefällen wimmelt. Bei so vielen Tücken ist vor allem eins gefragt: Ein gutes Gedächtnis.

➤ Konsonanten: Einer oder zwei?

ein Konsonant	zwei Konsonanten
metal – *Metall*	actually – *tatsächlich*
model – *Modell*	gradually – *allmählich*
rebel – *Rebell*	commit – *(ein Verbrechen) begehen*
emigrant – *Auswanderer/in*	immigrant – *Einwanderer/in*
telegram – *Telegramm*	annoy – *ärgern*
apartment – *Wohnung*	glass – *Glas*
career – *Karriere*	scissors – *(eine) Schere*

ein Konsonant plus zwei	zwei Konsonanten plus zwei
necessary – *notwendig*	accommodation – *Unterkunft*
parallel – *parallel*	access – *Zugang*
to disappear – *verschwinden*	success – *Erfolg*
to disappoint – *enttäuschen*	address – *Adresse, Anschrift*
	to assassinate – *ermorden*
	cassette – *Cassette*

➤ Konsonanten: Weitere Tücken

height – *Höhe;* where – *wo;* environment – *Umwelt;*
straight – *gerade;* whether – *ob;* government – *Regierung;*
belief, to believe – *Glaube, glauben;* proof, to prove – *Beweis, beweisen;*
life, to live – *Leben, leben;* safe, to save – *sicher, sparen, retten*

➤ **Nationalitätsbezeichnungen**

Land, Leute und Sprache werden immer **groß** geschrieben!
England, Englishman, English … American, Dutch, German, usw.

➤ **Zahlen**

four, fourteen, forty
five, fifteen, fifty, (the) fifth
eight, eighteen, eighty, (the) eighth,
twelve, (the) twelfth

Exam Tip 14 Im Gegensatz zum Deutschen fängt das erste Wort in der ersten Zeile in einem englischen Brief **groß** an:
Dear Joe,
***Thanks** for your letter …*

Exercise 1 Vervollständige die Sätze mit den englischen Übersetzungen.

1 How many ________________ were able to escape?
Rebellen

2 What's the difference between "____________________" and "____________________"? *Auswanderer, Einwanderer*

3 Her ________________ was a great ________________ .
Karriere, Erfolg

4 John F. Kennedy was ________________ in 1963. Why would anybody ________________ such a crime? *ermordet, begehen*

5 Lines which are ____________ must also be ____________ .
parallel, gerade

6 I'm not sure ______________ I can spell the words "________________" and "________________".
ob, Glaube, Beweis

7 What's ________________ times ______________ ?
vierzehn, vierzig

➤ -ise oder -ize?

Häufig ist die Endung -ise mit -ize austauschbar (realise und realize).
In wenigen Fällen kann man -ise **nicht** durch -ize ersetzen:
advertise – *Reklame machen*
advise – *(be)raten;* aber: advice – *Rat*
exercise, to exercise – *Übung; üben*
practise (BE) – *üben*
surprise, to surprise – *Überraschung, überraschen*
televise – *im Fernsehen übertragen*

➤ Ein Wort oder mehrere?

another – *ein(e); andere(r, s)*
cannot – *kann nicht*
despite – *trotz*
no one – *niemand*
in spite of – *trotz*

Exam Tip 15 Bei den Vorsilben ***anti-, ex-, pro-, self-*** ist ein Bindestrich immer notwendig, sowie bei Zahlen, ***thirty-two, sixty-five, …***
Merke dir folgende typische Zusammensetzungen:
*a **two-year-old** child; a **fifty-pound** note; a **fifteen-mile** walk;*
*a **well-known** author* (immer **mit** Bindestrich vor einem Substantiv).
Aber: *He is **well known**.*

Exercise 2 Richtig oder falsch? Bessere die falschen Sätze aus.

1 Marc has no selfconfidence inspite of the fact that he's a wellknown singer.
2 He's irish, sixty five years old and an ex-policeman.
3 People were surprised, even anoyed, to hear that sort of advise from the director, but noone realised that he was actualy joking.
4 I can not seriously believ that an other ten mile walk at the weekend will help me to loose weight, although I certainly need more exercize.
5 "Dear Dr West, you have been chosen to attend the UN-conference in Berlin as part of the UK-delegation …"

➤ Vokale mit Tücken

a
calendar – *Kalender;* **separate** – *getrennt;*
repeat – *wiederholen;* **cocoa** – *Kakao;*

i vor **c**
juice – *Saft*

ei nach **c**
ceiling – *Decke;* **receive** – *empfangen*

i vor **e** ausser vor **c**
chief – *Häuptling;* **niece** – *Nichte;* **thief** – *Dieb*

mit **e** / **ee**
aggressive – *aggressiv;* **satellite** – *Satellit;* **magazine** – *Zeitschrift;*
being (nur ein **e**!); **employee** – *Arbeitnehmer/in;*

ohne **e**
madam – *meine Dame (Anrede)*

➤ ... und noch ein paar Vokale zum Stolpern!

canoe – *Kanu*
cheque – *Scheck*
choir – *Chor*

colleague – *Kollege/-in*
dialogue – *Dialog*
medicine – *Medizin*

parliament – *Parlament*
poisonous – *giftig*
pronunciation – *Aussprache;*
aber: **to pronounce**

religious – *religiös*
queue – *Schlange (wartende Menschen); Schlange stehen*

➤ Groß oder klein?

Folgende Wörter werden immer groß geschrieben:
Catholic – *Katholik/in; katholisch*
Jewish – *jüdisch*
Muslim – *Moslem; moslemisch*
on Monday(s) – *am Montag, montags*
on Tuesday(s) – *am Dienstag, dienstags*

Exercise 3 Übersetze jeweils die farbigen Satzteile.

1 *Laut Kalender ist morgen Sonntag und sonntags schlafe ich immer länger.* ____________ it's ____________ tomorrow, and ____________ I always sleep longer.

2 *Zwei von meinen Kollegen singen im Chor.* ____________ ____________ sing ____________ .

3 *Es ist nur Medizin – es ist nichts Giftiges!*
It's only ____________ – it's nothing ____________ !

4 *Ist es eine jüdische oder eine moslemische Sitte?*
____________ custom?

5 *Der Dieb stahl zwei Schecks.* ____________ stole ____________ .

6 *Die Gäste saßen an getrennten Tischen.* The guests sat at ____________ .

Exercise 4 Übersetze die folgenden Wörter ins Englische (und benutze dabei nur dein Gedächtnis).

1 Kanu ____________

2 Decke ____________

3 empfangen ____________

4 Aussprache ____________

5 Schlange stehen ____________

6 Kakao ____________

7 Nichte ____________

8 verlieren ____________

Exam Tip 16 Schreibt man ***north, south, east, west*** klein oder groß?
Als Faustregel kann man sagen:
Groß, wenn man ein Gebiet bezeichnet sowie in Ländernamen
The USA leads ***the West****.* ***South Korea*** *…*
und **klein** in anderen Fällen *I'm travelling* ***north*** *tomorrow.*

➤ **-able oder -ible; -ant oder -ent; -ll oder -l?**

-able (nach Konsonaten und immer nach Vokalen, Vorsicht nach **e**!)
admirable – *bewundernswert* (to admire)
uncomfortable – *unbequem*
unimaginable – *unvorstellbar* (to imagine)
readable – *lesenswert*
recyclable – *wiederverwendbar* (to recycle)
valuable – *wertvoll* (to value)
reliable – *zuverlässig* (to rely)
Aber: unpronounc**e**able – *unaussprechbar*

-ible (weniger gebräuchlich – meistens nach **s**)
responsible – *verantwortlich;* visible – *sichtbar;* edible – *essbar*

-ant und -ent (diese Endungen muss man auswendig lernen)
assistant – *Assistent/in;*
confident – *(selbst)sicher;* efficient – *tüchtig;*
independent – *unabhängig;* violent – *gewalttätig*

-ll oder -l? (ein -l in der Endung -ful)
beautiful – *(wunder)schön;* careful – *sorgfältig;*
successful – *erfolgreich;* wonderful – *wunderbar*
Aber: till / until – *bis*

Exercise 5 Übersetze den ganzen Satz aus dem Gedächtnis.

1 *Das Wort ist fast unaussprechbar.*

____

2 *Die neue Assistentin ist zuverlässig, selbstsicher und tüchtig.*

____

3 *Claudia ist wunderschön und erfolgreich.*

____

4 *Warte bis ich komme.*

____

5 Der Plan ist bewundernswert, aber unvorstellbar. Bist du dafür verantwortlich? ______________________________

____

A 6 Einfacher oder doppelter Konsonant?

Streiche jeden Satz, in dem du einen Fehler findest.

1.1 I've planed a wonderfull party for tomorrow.
1.2 I've planned a wonderful party for tomorrow.
1.3 I've planed a wonderful party for tomorrow.

2.1 He admitted they had commited the crime.
2.2 He admited they had commited the crime.
2.3 He admited they had committed the crime.
2.4 He admitted they had committed the crime.

3.1 The patient is sufferring unimagineble pain.
3.2 The patient is sufferring unimaginable pain.
3.3 The patient is suffering unimaginable pain.
3.4 The patient is sufering unimaginable pain.

4.1 They haven't stopped quarrelling all day.
4.2 They haven't stoped quarelling all day.
4.3 They haven't stoped quareling all day.

5.1 The girls prefered to have seperate rooms.
5.2 The girls preferred to have seperate rooms.
5.3 The girls preferred to have separate rooms.

6.1 I've never regretted becoming self-employed *[selbstständig]*.
6.2 I've never regreted becoming selfemployed.
6.3 I've never regreted becoming self-employed.

Hast du das gekonnt?
Auch wenn du die Aufgabe vollständig richtig lösen konntest, **solltest du diesen wichtigen Abschnitt ganz durcharbeiten**.

Exam Tip 17 Wenn man im Deutschen **eine Unterkunft** sagt, redet man im Englischen fast immer von ***accommodation*** ohne ***a***.

Exam Tip 18 Die Liste von englischen Vokabeln, die als Stolpersteine gelten, ist schier endlos. Merke dir unter anderem:

biscuit – Keks, Plätzchen
to ***choose*** *(chose, chosen)* – (aus)wählen
delicious – köstlich, lecker
disaster – Katastrophe
discipline – Disziplin
official – offiziell
paid *(pay)* – bezahlen
queueing – Schlange stehen
science – (Natur)Wissenschaft
therefore – deswegen
through – durch
tough – zäh

Exam Tip 19 Als Vorbereitung auf den nächsten Test mache eine eigene Liste von Vokabeln, die für dich problematisch sind. Nur so kann man die Tücken der Rechtschreibung überwinden!

➤ Ein weiteres Rechtschreibproblem liegt bei den Verben. Schreibt man etwa to stop in der Vergangenheit (oder in der -ing-Form) mit einem p oder mit doppeltem p? Ähnlich verhält es sich bei sehr vielen gängigen Verben.

➤ **Der Endkonsonant wird verdoppelt bei:**

admi**t** → admi**tt**ed - *zugeben*
commi**t** (a crime) → commi**tt**ed - *begehen*
contro**l** → contro**ll**ed - *beherrschen*
dia**l**[1] (a number) → dia**ll**ed - *wählen*
fi**t** → fi**tt**ed - *passen*
permi**t** → permi**tt**ed - *erlauben*
pla**n** → pla**nn**ed - *planen*
prefe**r** → prefe**rr**ed - *lieber haben*
quarre**l** → quarre**ll**ed - *streiten*
regre**t** → regre**tt**ed - *bedauern*
ro**b** → ro**bb**ed - *berauben*
sto**p** → sto**pp**ed - *aufhören; anhalten*
trave**l**[1] → trave**ll**ed - *reisen*

[1]Im Amerikanischen heißt es dialed, traveled.

Aber:

develop	→ **developed** - *entwickeln*
offer	→ **offered** - *anbieten*
profit	→ **profited** - *profitieren*
suffer	→ **suffered** - *leiden*

➤ Als Faustregel gilt: Ist das vorhergehende **a, e, i, o, u** kurz bzw. betont, wird der Endkonsonant verdoppelt.

Exercise Richtig oder falsch? Bessere die falschen Sätze aus.

1 They were robed while they were travel(l)ing through Florida.

2 The firm is offerring me an other chance to be their officiall representative in London. I've been choosen from more than 100 candidates.

3 I can not imagine that the new dress fited her.

4 These biscuts are absolutely delicous.

5 We payed quite a lot to get into the Sciense Museum after we had been queuing for half an hour.

6 There's been a terrible desaster in an area South of here which is controlled by US-troops.

7 The West has profited from better relations with countries in the East.

8 She comes from a family of imigrants who emmigrated from Ireland in 1925.

9 They don't live at that address any longer.

10 There is no proove that King Arthur ever lifed.

A 7 Hilfsverben

Streiche jeden Satz, in dem du einen Fehler findest.

1.1 I like bird-watching very much.
1.2 Like you bird-watching?
1.3 Do you like bird-watching?

2.1 Who went to the party last weekend?
2.2 Who did go to the party last weekend?

3.1 Who ate the cat? The canary!
3.2 Who did the cat eat? The canary!

4.1 She can French.
4.2 She can speak French.
4.3 She does can French.

5.1 Bill wants to take his camera. So want I.
5.2 Bill wants to take his camera. So do I.
5.3 Bill wants to take his camera. I want, too.
5.4 Bill wants to take his camera. I do, too.

6.1 Jerry and Pat haven't had breakfast yet, and I haven't, too.
6.2 Jerry and Pat haven't had breakfast yet, and I hadn't too.
6.3 Jerry and Pat haven't had breakfast yet, and I haven't, either.
6.4 Jerry and Pat haven't had breakfast yet, and neither haven't I.
6.5 Jerry and Pat haven't had breakfast yet, and neither have I.

7.1 They eat breakfast in bed every day, not true?
7.2 They eat breakfast in bed every day, or?
7.3 They eat breakfast in bed every day, don't they?
7.4 They eat breakfast in bed every day, aren't they?

8.1 We haven't got enough time, haven't we?
8.2 We haven't got enough time, no?
8.3 We haven't got enough time, have we?
8.4 We haven't got enough time, do we?

Hast du das gekonnt?
Falls du nicht alle falschen Sätze identifiziert hast, mach weiter mit diesem Abschnitt (Seite 37).
Falls du die Aufgabe richtig lösen konntest, mach weiter mit dem nächsten Abschnitt (Seite 40).

➤ Hilfsverben haben im Englischen eine wichtigere und vielfältigere Funktion als im Deutschen.

➤ **Sie werden gebraucht** …

… zusammen mit einem Vollverb um die Bedeutung zu ergänzen:
She **can** play the cello.
It **might** rain tomorrow.
You **shouldn't** stay in the sun too long.

… in Aussagesätzen um die Zeitformen auszudrücken:
They **have** already seen that film.
Susan **will** help us with the party.

Ausnahme!
Bei Aussagesätzen in einfacher Gegenwart und Vergangenheit ist kein Hilfsverb nötig:
He likes Pizza. Mary and John went to Paris.

… in der Regel um Fragen zu bilden:
Do you like pizza? Where **did** they go?

Ausnahme!
Kein Hilfsverb bei einfacher Gegenwart und Vergangenheit, wenn nach dem Subjekt gefragt wird:
Who likes pizza? How many people went to Rome?

… um Verneinungen zu bilden.
He **doesn't** like pizza. They **didn't** go there.

… bei Kurzantworten ohne Vollverb:
Has he met her? Yes, he **has**.
Who likes artichokes? John **does**, but Ruth **doesn't**.

… um Gemeinsamkeiten auszudrücken, nach folgendem Muster:
Jim can play tennis. Mary **can**, too. / So **can** Mary. – *Mary auch.*
I've seen that film. I **have**, too. / So **have** I. – *Ich auch.*
I don't like beer. Jo **doesn't**, either. / Neither **does** Jo. – *Jo auch nicht.*

… als Frageanhängsel, entsprechend dem Deutschen „nicht wahr? / oder?" nach folgendem Muster:
Jim **can** play tennis, **can't** he?
You've seen that film, **haven't** you?
He **doesn't** like beer, **does** he?

······· **Exam Tip 20** *Can* wird **nie** als Vollverb benutzt!

Exercise Übersetze die deutschen Sätze.

1 *Er mag keine Hamburger und Jane auch nicht.*

___

2 *Was isst du jeden Tag zum Frühstück? Wer macht dein Frühstück?*

___

___

3 *Wie viele Leute möchten ins Konzert? Wie viel kosten die Karten?*

___

___

4 *Kannst du Französisch?*

___

5 *Ja, ich spreche Französisch. Traudl auch. Aber Bruce nicht. Und Mark auch nicht.*

___

___

6 *Sie ist sehr freundlich, nicht wahr?*

___

7 *Wir haben noch nicht genug bezahlt, oder?*

___

8 *Wir sollten nicht mit den Auto fahren, oder?*

___

9 *Er fährt jeden Tag zur Arbeit, nicht wahr?*

___

10 *Sie haben einige Fehler gemacht, nicht wahr?*

___

___

B

B 1 Simple present oder present progressive?

Streiche jeden Satz, in dem du einen Fehler findest.

1.1 We usually spend our summer holidays at the seaside.
1.2 We are usually spending our summer holidays at the seaside.

Why is he in New York?

2.1 He's interviewing Broadway musical stars for his new book.
2.2 He interviews Broadway musical stars for his new book.

3.1 He isn't liking avocados.
3.2 He doesn't like avocados.

Please give this to Mimi.

4.1 She's repairing the washing machine in the bathroom.
4.2 She repairs the washing machine in the bathroom.

Let me check the schedule.

5.1 Yes, Flight BA 76 arrives in Paris at 14.50. Shall I book the flight?
5.2 Yes, Flight BA 76 is arriving in Paris at 14.50. Shall I book the flight?

6.1 I have a party this weekend. Would you like to come?
6.2 I'm having a party this weekend. Would you like to come?

7.1 Sorry, I can't give you my CD player. John is using it for his party.
7.2 Sorry, I can't give you my CD player. John uses it for his party.

8.1 I talked to her yesterday. She thinks the sofa is a terrible colour.
8.2 I talked to her yesterday. She's thinking the sofa is a terrible colour.

9.1 She's thinking of buying another one.
9.2 She thinks of buying another one.

10.1 Dr No? Is that the James Bond film where he fights the dragon?
10.2 Dr No? Is that the James Bond film where he is fighting the dragon?

11.1 Hey! What are you doing with my hat? Stop!
11.2 Hey! What do you do with my hat? Stop!

Hast du das gekonnt?
Falls du nicht alle falschen Sätze identifiziert hast, mache weiter mit diesem Abschnitt (Seite 41).
Falls du die Aufgabe richtig lösen konntest, mache weiter mit dem nächsten Abschnitt (Seite 43).

➤ Da es im Deutschen keine unterschiedlichen einfachen (simple) und Verlaufs-Verbformen (progressive) gibt, haben Englischlernende oft Probleme mit diesem Konzept, das auf allen Zeitstufen vorkommt. Es gibt jedoch Regeln und Anhaltspunkte, die einem weiterhelfen. Beginnen wir mit den zwei Gegenwartsformen.

➤ **Das simple present wird benutzt** …

… für gewohnheitsmäßige Handlungen und feststehende Tatsachen:
I usually **drink** orange juice for breakfast.

… für künftiges Geschehen, festgelegt im Fahrplan oder Stundenplan:
The tour bus **leaves** the hotel at 9 pm tomorrow.

… um eine Handlung in einer Geschichte, Film, Brief, etc. zu beschreiben:
In this story, Pecos Pete **robs** the bank and **gives** the money to his sick mother.

➤ **Das present progressive wird benutzt für** …

… einen Vorgang, der gerade abläuft oder von begrenzten Dauer ist:
What'**s** Kim **doing** in the kitchen? She'**s making** pizza.
I'**m driving** to work with a colleague this week.

… für feste Absichten in der Zukunft, bei denen die Planung schon abgeschlossen ist.
I'**m babysitting** for our neighbour next Friday, but I'**m** not **doing** anything special on Saturday.

Exam Tip 21 Bei *present simple* nicht vergessen: *He, she, it* – das *s* muss mit!

Exercise 1 Setze die richtigen Verbformen ein.

That's Fay Jones, from Conway Computers. She has a good job. She ____________ help customers find the best system for their company, and ____________ teach them how to use new programmes. She usually ____________ travel a lot. This week she's in London. She ____________ train employees for a very big company there.

Next month she ______________ → attend → a trade fair *[Messe]* in Atlanta, and ______________ → give → presentations of the newest systems. It's a difficult trip for her, because the plane ______________ → arrive → in Atlanta at 2.20 pm. And her first presentation is at 4.pm ! Her boyfriend never ______________ → travel → with her, and he isn't very happy about her job. It's like in that film, where the woman ______________ → have → an interesting career, but finally ______________ → lose → her husband.

➤ Vorsicht! Verben, die Meinungen wie **believe, like, think, know,** Sinneswahrnehmungen wie **see,** Besitz wie **have,** Sein wie **be,** und Wollen wie **want** ausdrücken, werden in der Regel **nicht** in der progressiven Form verwendet.

➤ Dabei muss beachtet werden, dass einige Wörter verschiedene Bedeutungen haben können, wie z.B. **have** und **think**:

I **have** a new bicycle. – *haben*
We'**re having** our English class. – *durchführen*
He'**s having** a good time. – *erleben*
I **think** she's very nice. – *meinen*
I'**m thinking** about the problem. – *überlegen*

Exercise 2 Setze die richtigen Verbformen ein.

Fay's mother ______________ → think → Fay works too hard. She often ______________ → tell → her that she'll never get a husband. At the moment she ______________ → try → to get Fay to plan her wedding. Fay ______________ → has → a terrible time with her just now. She ______________ → think → of getting a new phone number and not giving it to her. Fay ______________ → love → her mother and her boyfriend, but she ______________ → not / want → a husband now, not for a few years anyway! She ______________ → have → an interesting job, and ______________ → believe → there will be plenty of time later for a family.

B 2 Present oder present perfect progressive?

Streiche jeden Satz, in dem du einen Fehler findest.

1.1 I am living in Munich since 1973.
1.2 I have been living in Munich since 1973.
1.3 I live in Munich since 1973.
1.4 I have lived in Munich since 1973.

2.1 How long have you been playing tennis? Since my childhood.
2.2 How long are you playing tennis? Since my childhood.
2.3 How long do you play tennis? Since my childhood.

3.1 She's been working in the hot kitchen for hours.
3.2 She's been working in the hot kitchen since hours.
3.3 She's working in the hot kitchen since hours.

4.1 I haven't seen her for years.
4.2 I haven't seen her since years.
4.3 I am not seeing her since years.

5.1 I have known her all my life.
5.2 I know her all my life.
5.3 I have been knowing her all my life.

Hast du das gekonnt?
Falls du nicht alle falschen Sätze identifiziert hast, mache weiter mit diesem Abschnitt (Seite 44). Falls du die Aufgabe richtig lösen konntest, kannst du mit dem nächsten Abschnitt (Seite 46) weitermachen.

➤ Einer der häufigsten Fehler im Gebrauch von Zeitformen ist die Verwechslung des present und des present perfect.
Das present perfect ist im Englischen keine reine Vergangenheitsform. Wenn der Zeitraum eine Verbindung zwischen Vergangenheit und Gegenwart herstellt, darf im Englischen nur das present perfect, in der Regel in der Verlaufsform, benutzt werden.

Hier geht es mit present:
Ich suche eine Arbeit. I'**m looking** for a new job.
Meine Mutter ist Lehrerin. My mother **is** a teacher.

Aber hier ist nur present perfect möglich:
Ich suche seit Mai eine Arbeit. I **have been looking** for a job since May.
Sie ist seit 12 Jahren Lehrerin. She **has been** a teacher for 12 years.

➤ Auf die Frage How long has it been happening?
machen wir eine Zeitangabe mit

since um den Zeitpunkt, seit wann eine Handlung oder ein Zustand andauert, zu kennzeichnen: **since** March, **since** I came here, **since** my birth, **since** 1990, …

for um den Zeitraum, in dem sich die Handlung abspielt, zu kennzeichnen: **for** 3 months, **for** years, **for** ages, …

➤ Beachte! Es gibt Verben, die in der Regel nie in der Verlaufsform stehen, vgl. B1, Seite 42. Anstelle der Verlaufsform wird das present perfect simple benutzt:
I **haven't seen** you since 1992! She'**s loved** him for years.

➤ Die Verben **live** und **work** können sowohl in der einfachen Form (simple) wie auch in der Verlaufsform (progressive) gebraucht werden:
I **live** in Sweden. / I'**m living** in Sweden.
I **have lived** in Sweden for five years. / I **have been living** in Sweden for five years.

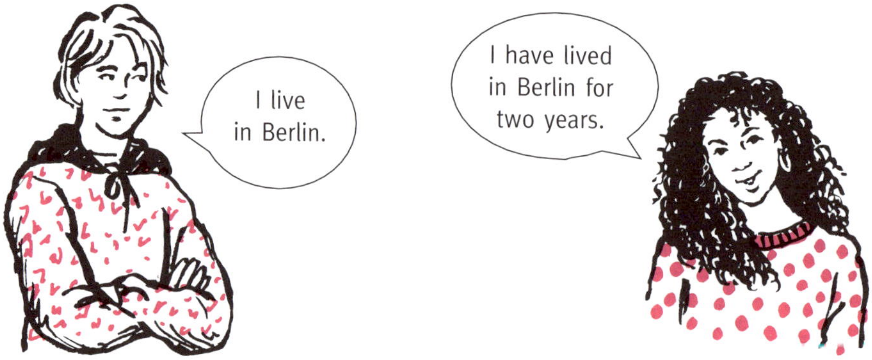

Exercise Übersetze den ganzen Satz.

1 *Tom und Jerry spielen Poker.*

2 *Wie lange spielen sie schon Poker?*

3 *Ich bin erschöpft. Seit heute früh um sieben streiche ich die Küche.*

4 *Ich wohne in Kairo.*

5 *Ach, wirklich? Wie lange wohnen Sie schon dort?*

6 *Stimmt das wirklich? Seit Jahren denke ich, dass sie seine Sekretärin ist.*

7 *Ist es noch nicht fertig? Er arbeitet schon ewig an diesem alten Haus.*

8 *Natürlich kenne ich ihn. Ich kenne ihn seit Jahren.*

9 *Wie lange bist du schon hier in Florenz?*

10 *Ich spiele noch nicht lange Klavier. Erst seit März.*

B 3 Simple past oder past progressive?

Streiche jeden Satz, in dem du einen Fehler findest.

1.1 I couldn't hear the phone when you called. I was washing my hair.
1.2 I couldn't hear the phone when you called. I washed my hair then.

The murder happened at 8 o'clock this morning.
2.1 What did you do at that time?
2.2 What were you doing at that time?

He asked me if I wanted to go to Australia with them.
3.1 What did you answer?
3.2 Really? What were you answering?

4.1 At this time yesterday we were studying English.
4.2 At this time last year we studied English.

5.1 He took a picture of the tiger, then went home and had dinner.
5.2 He was taking a picture of the tiger, then was going home and having dinner.

6.1 He was having dinner when we came to see him. So we waited.
6.2 He was having dinner when we came to see him. So we were waiting.
6.3 He had dinner when we came to see him. So we waited.
6.4 He had dinner when we came to see him. So we were waiting.

Hast du das gekonnt? Falls du nicht alle falschen Sätze identifiziert hast, mache weiter mit diesem Abschnitt (Seite 46). Ansonsten kannst du zum nächsten Abschnitt (Seite 48) gehen.

- Das simple past (einfache Vergangenheit) wird verwendet, um zu berichten, dass etwas zu einer bestimmten Zeit in der Vergangenheit passiert und abgeschlossen ist.
  Pecos Pete **put** on his hat, **walked** out of the door, and never **returned**.
- Das past progressive (Verlaufsform der Vergangenheit) wird verwendet, um zu erzählen, was gerade im Gange war, als etwas anderes geschah, oder zu einer bestimmten Zeit in der Vergangenheit für einige Zeit geschehen ist.
  I **was having** a shower when the doorbell rang.
  I **was living** in Seattle then.
- Vergiss nie die Verben, die nicht in der Verlaufsform stehen; vgl. Seite 42.

Exercise Markiere die jeweils passende Zeitform.

On Friday afternoon, Mrs Gill *baked / was baking* six chocolate cakes for Saturday afternoon tea at her small hotel. At 5 o'clock she *put / was putting* them in the pantry and *went / was going* shopping. When she *came / was coming* back at 6.30, the cakes were gone! "Somebody *stole / was stealing* my cakes while I *shopped / was shopping*!" she cried. But who? A lot of guests *stayed / were staying* at the hotel that weekend, but most of them *watched / were watching* a golf tournament nearby, when the cakes were stolen. Only three guests were at the hotel Friday afternoon. She politely *asked / was asking* them to come to the kitchen. "Sorry to bother you," she said, "but, could you please tell me, what you *did / were doing* between 5 o'clock and 6.30?" Mrs Jones said: Mr Kildare, here, and I *played / were playing* cards upstairs. We *finished / were finishing* at about 7. Peg Smith's parents were at the tournament. "I *came / was coming* into the kitchen to get something to drink." said Peg. "While I was there your neighbour *knocked / was knocking* at the window, and said she had come for the cakes for the school fete. So I *gave / was giving* them to her. They *looked / were looking very good*!" "Oh no," said Mrs Gill. "there's no school fete."

B 4 Present perfect oder simple past?

Streiche jeden Satz, in dem du einen Fehler findest.

1.1 Have you seen that film yet?
1.2 Have you gone with the class to that film yersterday?

2.1 I called him yesterday morning.
2.2 I've called him yesterday morning.

3.1 I've never been to Rio for the Carnival.
3.2 I never went to Rio for the Carnival.

4.1 I can't eat anything. I've just come from the dentist.
4.2 I can't eat anything. I just came from the dentist.

5.1 Have you ever seen a purple cow?
5.2 Did you ever see a purple cow?

6.1 I've lived in Grossdingharting all my life.
6.2 I lived in Grossdingharting all my life.

7.1 He played the piano often when he was a child.
7.2 He has played the piano often when he was a child.

8.1 They haven't gone fishing recently.
8.2 They didn't go fishing recently.

9.1 After they made her sales manager, she started travelling a lot.
9.2 After they have made her sales manager, she's started travelling a lot.

10.1 I've often started to keep a diary, but I've never got very far.
10.2 I often started to keep a diary, but I never got very far.

11.1 I've been to Scotland several times.
11.2 I've been to Scotland last in June.

Hast du das gekonnt?
Falls du nicht alle falschen Sätze identifiziert hast, mache weiter mit diesem Abschnitt (Seite 49).

Falls du die Aufgabe richtig lösen konntest, mache weiter mit dem nächsten Abschnitt (Seite 51).

➤ Beim present perfect besteht das Problem, dass es zu häufig verwendet wird. Es wird im Englischen nie für abgeschlossene Handlungen, die zu einem bekannten Zeitpunkt geschehen sind, gebraucht. Hier kommt nur das simple past in Frage:

They **went** to New Zealand last June for their holidays.
We often **went** to the beach when we lived in California.

➤ Das present perfect benutzt man für Handlungen in einem Zeitraum, der noch nicht genau festgelegt ist, oder noch nicht abgeschlossen ist. Es kommt häufig mit Wörtern wie **already**, **ever**, **never**, **just**, **recently**, **yet** vor:

We'**ve** already **done** our shopping this week.
He'**s** just **arrived.**
He **hasn't seen** his friends recently.
Have you ever **ridden** a camel? No, **I've** never **done** that.
Yes, **I've ridden** a camel five or six times.

Exercise Ist das Verb im *present perfect* richtig oder falsch? Wenn es falsch ist, musst du das Verb ins *simple past* setzen.

Dear Mr Jameson,

I'm very interested in the job of au pair,

as advertised in The European.

Last week Mr Jones from the agency

____

has told me that you

____

haven't found anybody for the job yet.

I ______________________ have finished my A-levels in June 1996 and the following September I ______________________

have started a commercial correspondence course at a private college in our city. Unfortunately, the college ______________________

__________ has been forced to close at the end of the year,

Jutta Sailer
Gartens
71229

because of financial difficulties and I ________________________ haven't been able to complete my studies, yet.

As I cannot begin a course which interests me for another year, I ________________________ have decided this would be a good time to improve my knowledge of English and get valuable experience living in another country by doing something which I ________________________ have always enjoyed – taking care of children.

I ________________________ have never lived abroad, but I ________________________ have had a lot of experience with children.

From January to June last year, I ________________________ have worked part time at a kindergarten in our town.

That summer, I ________________________ have lived with a family in the north of Germany, and ________________________ have taken care of their three children, ages four, six and nine.

I ________________________ have enjoyed my stay with them very much, and they ________________________ have invited me to work for them again, next summer but I would prefer to have the experience of working abroad.

Both this family and the head of the kindergarten ________________________ have written references for me, and I am enclosing them with this letter.

Since the summer holidays, I ________________________ have had several babysitting jobs, for children aged 6 months to 10 years old. I have got a valid driving licence and

B 5 Present perfect simple oder progressive?

Streiche jeden Satz, in dem du einen Fehler findest.

1.1 I've just cut my finger.
1.2 I've just been cutting my finger.

2.1 How long have you been living in Munich?
2.2 How long have you lived in Munich?

3.1 He's been being our sales representative for 13 years now.
3.2 He's been our sales representative for 13 years now.

4.1 I haven't seen the film *Independence Day* yet.
4.2 I haven't been seeing the film *Independence Day* yet.

5.1 We've just been having breakfast. Would you like to join us for some?
5.2 We've just had breakfast. Would you like to join us for some?

6.1 Thanks. I haven't been having breakfast yet.
6.2 Thanks. I haven't had breakfast yet.

7.1 We've already had our meeting about that project.
7.2 We've already been having our meeting about that project.

8.1 We've been having meetings about that project since January.
8.2 We've had meetings about that project since January.

9.1 I'm afraid I've hit your car.
9.2 I'm afraid I've been hitting your car.

10.1 They haven't lived there for a long time. They've moved.
10.2 They haven't lived there for a long time. They've been moving.

You look very hot and tired.
11.1 Yes. We've been working very hard in the garden.
11.2 Yes, we've worked very hard in the garden.

Hast du das gekonnt?
Falls du nicht alle falschen Sätze identifiziert hast, mache weiter mit diesem Abschnitt (Seite 52). Falls du die Aufgabe richtig lösen konntest, mache weiter mit dem nächsten Abschnitt (Seite 54).

➤ Beide Formen, das present perfect simple und das present perfect continuous haben Folgendes gemeinsam: die Handlung vollzieht sich in der Vergangenheit und schließt die Gegenwart ein.

Der Unterschied liegt darin, dass beim present perfect simple die Handlung schon vollzogen, der genaue Zeitpunkt jedoch unbestimmt ist:
Have you ever **used** a computer?
He'**s** already **read** the newspaper (this morning / today).

➤ Beim present perfect continuous setzt sich die Handlung, die in der Vergangenheit begonnen hat, bis in die Gegenwart fort.
She'**s been using** her computer since January… (*Und wird es noch weiter tun.*)
You'**ve been reading** my paper for an hour. Could I please have it back?

Möglich ist auch, dass die Handlung beendet ist, die Folgen aber noch spürbar sind.
She looks really tired. Yes, she'**s been working** very hard since 6 this morning.

Beim present perfect continuous wird der Ausgangspunkt oft mit **since** oder **for** bezeichnet.

➤ Beachte: Die Verben **live** and **work** sind Ausnahmen und können in der einfachen Form dieselbe Bedeutung haben wie in der Verlaufsform:
They **have lived / have been living** in that house for thirty years.

➤ Vergiss nie die Verben, die nicht in der Verlaufsform stehen, vgl. Seite 42.

Exercise Markiere die jeweils passende Zeitform.

1 Have you got a bandage? I've *burnt / been burning* my hand.

2 She's *worked / been working* for our company since 1993.

3 Look, it's half past six. How long have they *played / been playing* tennis?

4 What's the matter with him? He looks awful. Yes. He's *looked / been looking* after his two nephews.

5 Sorry, I can't take that. I've already *packed / been packing* my bags.

6 Have you *known / been knowing* her for a long time?

7 I've never *done / been doing* any rock climbing.

8 We've painted / been painting the kitchen since 6 am. It's time for a break.

9 Where have they *learned / been learning* judo? At the YMCA. I think their course for beginners finishes next week.

10 I've *written / been writing* the letter, but I haven't *sent / been sending* it yet.

B 6 Let, make, get / have something done

Streiche jeden Satz, in dem du einen Fehler findest.

1.1 I haven't got much time, so I always let my shirts ironed.
1.2 I haven't got much time, so I always get my shirts ironed.
1.3 I haven't got much time, so I always have my shirts ironed.

2.1 We should really get Mary to do the decorations. She's the best.
2.2 We should really let Mary to do the decorations. She's the best.
2.3 We should really have Mary to do the decorations. She's the best.
2.4 We should really have Mary do the decorations. She's the best.

3.1 When I was little my parents always made me go to bed at 7 o'clock. I hated it.
3.2 When I was little my parents always let me go to bed at 7 o'clock. I hated it.

4.1 I let my own children stay up much later.
4.2 I make my own children stay up much later.

5.1 I usually have my hair cut once a month.
5.2 I usually get my hair cut once a month.
5.3 I usually let my hair cut once a month.
5.4 I usually have cut my hair once a month.

6.1 I have already repaired my toaster myself.
6.2 I have already my toaster repaired myself.

Hast du das gekonnt?
Falls du nicht alle falschen Sätze identifiziert hast, mache weiter mit diesen Abschnitt (Seite 55).
Falls du die Aufgabe richtig lösen konntest, mache weiter mit dem nächsten Abschnitt (Seite 57).

➤ Jemanden etwas machen lassen im Sinne von „etwas zulassen" oder „etwas erlauben" wird im Englischen entweder mit **let somebody do something** oder mit **allow somebody to do something** ausgedrückt:
I **didn't let the police look** in the bedroom.
They **allowed me to talk** to the prisoner for fifteen minutes.

➤ „Jemanden veranlassen, etwas zu tun" wird im Englischen mit **have someone do something** oder mit **get somebody to do something** wiedergegeben:
When I was little my mother **had me ring** my father once a week.
You should **get Mary to help** you study for the exam. She's really good.

➤ „Jemanden dazu zwingen oder bringen, etwas zu tun", wird ausgedrückt mit **make somebody do something**.
Im Passiv wird dieser Ausdruck mit **to + Infinitiv** verwendet:
I **made him clean up** his own mess.
I **was made to do** things like that when I was a child, too.

➤ „Etwas machen lassen", d.h. veranlassen, dass etwas von jemandem getan wird, heißt **have something done**.
Achte auf die Wortstellung. Das Partizip Perfekt steht **nach** dem Objekt:
I **have** the windows **cleaned**. – *Ich lasse meine Fenster putzen.*

Wenn das Objekt nach dem Partizip Perfekt steht, ist das nur ein Satz im present perfect:
I **have washed** my windows. – *Ich habe meine Fenster geputzt.*

Exercise Übersetze die fehlenden Satzteile.

I really like my new job at the fitness farm. There's a very relaxed atmosphere. *Die zwingen uns nicht* ______________________________ __________ wear awful uniforms like in my last job. We can wear what we like. Do you remember how *wir gezwungen wurden* _____________ ______________________ work overtime almost every evening in my last job? Here they have enough staff, and they *lassen uns gehen* __________________________________ home early, quite often. And they *erlauben uns* ________________________ use the swimming pool and the fitness centre during our lunch break.

I often prefer that to eating, and anyway we can *das Personal veranlassen, uns einen Imbiss und Kaffee zu bringen* ______________

____

during our afternoon break. Yesterday I *habe meinen Rücken und meine Füße massieren lassen* ____________________________

__________________________ for no money at all. You know at the last place *sie haben uns zahlen lassen* ________________________

________________________________ , if we wanted *es machen lassen* ____ .

Here they like to *die neuen Mitarbeiter üben lassen* _______________

_____________________________ on the personnel to get a lot of experience. And there's a woman who does astrology, too. *Ich werde mein Horoskop nächste Woche machen lassen.* ________________

____ .

You should *sie veranlassen, deines auch zu machen* _______________

____ . She could use the extra work, and it's very interesting. I'll *veranlasse sie, dich nächste Woche anzurufen* ___________________________________

________________ to make an appointment.

B 7 Shall, should, be supposed to, ought to, had better

Streiche jeden Satz, in dem du einen Fehler findest.

1.1 He shall do exercises every morning, but he never does.
1.2 He is supposed to do exercises every morning, but he never does.

2.1 I should call my mother, but that's OK, it's not all that important.
2.2 I shall call my mother, but that's OK, it's not all that important.
2.3 I had better call my mother, but that's OK, it's not all that important.

Our business meeting starts early tomorrow.
3.1 I really should go home now.
3.2 I really ought to go to bed now.
3.3 I'm supposed to go to bed now.

4.1 Don't forget. You ought to turn off the machine before you go.
4.2 Don't forget. You're supposed to turn off the machine before you go.
4.3 Don't forget. You should turn off the machine before you go. It's essential.

I'd really like to help you with your party.
5.1 Shall I come early and help you with the decorations?
5.2 Am I supposed to come early and help you with the decorations?

There are a lot of bears in this national park.
6.1 You had better not keep food in your tent.
6.2 You shall better not keep food in your tent.

7.1 They are said to have a lot of thunderstorms in this area.
7.2 They ought to have a lot of thunderstorms in this area.
7.3 They shall have a lot of thunderstorms in this area.

Hast du das gekonnt? Falls du nicht alle falschen Sätze identifiziert hast, mach weiter mit diesem Abschnitt (Seite 58). Ansonsten kannst du zum nächsten Abschnitt (Seite 60) gehen.

- **Shall** wird hauptsächlich für Angebote, Vorschläge und Bitten um Vorschläge verwendet. Seltener wird shall statt will zum Ausdruck der Zukunft mit I oder we benutzt.

  In anderen Fällen wird das deutsche Wort „sollen“ nicht mit shall übersetzt. Hier sind einige wichtige Beispiele, die unterschiedliche Grade von Dringlichkeit ausdrücken.

- **Ought to** and **should** können fast immer für allgemeinen Ratschlägen und Aufforderungen benutzt werden.
  You **ought to** / **should** see a doctor about that cough.

- Mit **had better** ist der Ratschlag dringender, fast eine Warnung.
  You **had better** not go swimming there. It's very dangerous.

- **Be supposed to** verwendet man für Mitteilungen, Anweisungen, Aufforderungen oder Ratschläge, wenn diese Aussagen von anderen Personen stammen.
  (The doctor says) I'**m supposed to** stay in bed until Tuesday.

  Be supposed to, wie **be said** / **considered to be**, kann auch ausdrücken das etwas **angeblich** der Fall sein soll.
  He'**s supposed to** be (**said to be**) a millionaire, but I don't believe it!

Exam Tip 22 Never *to* after ***had better*** and ***should***!

Exercise Vervollständige die Sätze mit einer passenden Entsprechung für „sollen“.

1 You ________________ *sollen nicht* ski there. There are avalanche warnings for that area.

2 She says you ________________ take this medicine every three hours.

3 You look tired. ________________ I wash the dishes for you?

4 The boss left a message for you. You ________________ type these letters. When they're finished, you ________________ ________ to take them to him for his signature, then put them in the post.

5 You ________________ ask him for the money if you need it that badly. He ____________________ to be very rich.

6 The train looks crowded. ____________________ we wait for the next one?

7 It's her birthday. We ___________________ buy her some flowers.

Dear Alison,
Come to my birthday party!
Wednesday, 9th September, 7 o'clock.
Margret

B8 Used to do, used to doing, get used to

Streiche jeden Satz, in dem du einen Fehler findest.

1.1 I get up every morning at 6.30, but I'm used to doing it now.
1.2 I get up every morning at 6.30, but I used to do it now.

2.1 When I was a student I used to often eat in that restaurant.
2.2 When I was a student I'm used to eating in that restaurant.
2.3 When I was a student I would often eat in that restaurant.

3.1 I used to call him yesterday.
3.2 I called him yesterday.

4.1 Call the office. She is used to go there early on Mondays.
4.2 Call the office. She usually goes there early on Mondays.

5.1 Did you use to live in Oxford?
5.2 Did you live in Oxford in former times?
5.3 Did you early live in Oxford?

6.1 I used to meet a famous film star on my holiday last summer.
6.2 I met a famous film star on my holiday last summer.

7.1 I didn't used to like coffee, but now I do.
7.2 I usedn't to like coffee, but I do now.
7.3 I didn't use to like coffee, but I do now.
7.4 I'm not used to liking coffee, but I do now.

8.1 The water's cold, but you can get used to it quickly.
8.2 The water's cold but you can get use to it quickly.
8.3 The water's cold, but you used to get it quickly.

9.1 I'm getting used to living alone.
9.2 I'm getting used to live alone.
9.3 I'm getting use to living alone.
9.4 I'm used to living alone.

Hast du das gekonnt?
Falls du nicht alle falschen Sätze identifiziert hast,
mache weiter mit diesem Abschnitt (Seite 61).
Falls du die Aufgabe richtig lösen konntest,
mache weiter mit dem nächsten Abschnitt (Seite 63).

➤ Oft verwechselt werden drei wichtige englische Strukturen, die mit **used to** gebildet werden.

Mit **used to** + **Infinitiv** (Grundform) des Vollverbs berichtest du über frühere Zustände, Gewohnheiten oder regelmäßige, wiederholte Handlungen.
Letzteres wird auch manchmal mit **would** + **Infinitiv** ausgedrückt:
She **used to be** a famous filmstar and **live** in an expensive house.
Sie war früher ein berühmter Filmstar und wohnte in einem teuren Haus.
She **used to make** (**would make**) four or five films a year in those days.
Sie pflegte damals, vier bis fünf Filme pro Jahr zu machen.

➤ Während es sich oben nur um Vergangenes handelt, handelt es sich bei **be + used to** + **-ing-Form** des Verbs um etwas, an das man gewöhnt ist:
I'**m** not **used to getting** up early.
Ich bin nicht daran gewöhnt, früh aufzustehen.

➤ **Get + used to** + **-ing-Form** bedeutet, dass man sich an etwas gewöhnen wird:
He **is used to getting** up early, but he can't **get used to eating** a big breakfast then.
Er ist daran gewöhnt, früh aufzustehen, aber er kann sich nicht daran gewöhnen, so früh ein großes Frühstück zu essen.

Exercise Ergänze die Sätze mit einer Form des angegebenen Verbs in der einfachen Vergangenheit oder einer **used to**-Form, wo es passt.

My friends, John and Mabel Potts, live in Feelham in London now. He works in a bank and she's a nurse. They like their jobs, and they always find a lot of interesting things to do in the city in their free time. But until 1990 they *haben* ______________________ a very different life. They *wohnen* ______________________ and *arbeiten* ______________________ on their family farm in Sussex. Now they *nicht gewohnt / arbeiten* ______________________ more than forty hours a week, but on the farm they *arbeiten* ______________________ much more than that, especially during the summer.

"We never *haben* __________________ a proper holiday." says Mabel. "Many of our friends *gehen* __________________ off to the seaside, or *reisen* __________________ to Europe during the summer holidays. We *immer tun müssen* ______________________ our heaviest work then."

"But there *sein* ______________________ a lot things we loved about our life then, too," adds John. "The countryside was beautiful, and we still *nicht gewohnt / leben* ______________________ in all this dirty air and noise. The main reason we *verlassen* ______________________ the farm, was that I *haben* ______________________ a heart attack *[Herzinfarkt]* and couldn't do such heavy work anymore. So we *verkaufen* __________________ the farm and *umziehen* ______________________ to the city. Mabel *sein* ________________ a nurse in a hospital near the farm before she *heiraten* ______________________ me, and she *sein* ____________________ happy to go back to that job again."

"I really loved the farm," says Mabel, "But, I never *mich gewöhnen können / melken* ____________________ the cows, and *füttern* ______________________ the chicken every morning. Those were my jobs then."

B 9 Gerundium oder Infinitiv

Streiche jeden Satz, in dem du einen Fehler findest.

1.1 I can't imagine to give up smoking.
1.2 I can't imagine giving up smoking.
1.3 I can't imagine giving up to smoke.

2.1 We suggested to look for a new secretary.
2.2 We suggested to looking for a new secretary.
2.3 We suggested looking for a new secretary.

3.1 Jakob wishes to study medicine and becoming a doctor.
3.2 Jakob wishes studying medicine and becoming a doctor.
3.3 Jakob wishes to study medicine and become a doctor.

4.1 The boss would like to speak to you now.
4.2 The boss would like speaking to you now.
4.3 The boss would like to speaking to you now.

5.1 Is Russian really worth to learn?
5.2 Is Russian really worth being learned?
5.3 Is Russian really worth learning?

6.1 When did you start working here?
6.2 When did you start to work here?
6.3 When did you start to working here?

7.1 I began doing this job last summer.
7.2 I began to do this job last summer.
7.3 I began at doing this job last summer.

8.1 Have you ever practised to play the guitar?
8.2 Have you ever practised playing the guitar?
8.3 Have you ever practised at playing the guitar?

Hast du das gekonnt?
Falls du nicht alle falschen Sätze identifiziert hast, mache weiter mit diesem Abschnitt (Seite 64).
Falls du die Aufgabe richtig lösen konntest, mache weiter mit dem nächsten Abschnitt (Seite 68).

Exam Tip 23 Nach den Verben ***remember*** und ***forget*** steht immer ein **Infinitiv** oder **Gerundium** und nicht *remember / forget + how ...*
z.B.: Ich erinnere mich, wie ich L.A. um ersten Mal sah. –
*I **remember seeing** L.A. for the first time.*

➤ Ein Gerundium endet auf -ing

smoking ↔ to smoke; **talking** ↔ to talk;
und kann als Subjekt eines Satzes benutzt werden z.B.:
The **sinking** of the ship was a crime. –
Das Versenken des Schiffes war ein Verbrechen.
Das Gerundium steht nach einer Reihe von gängigen Verben als Objekt. Diese Verben solltest du auswendig lernen kann. Die Wahl zwischen Infinitiv und Gerundium nach diesen Verben und Ausdrücken ist deshalb einfach, denn die Kombinationen stehen fest.

➤ Verben + -ing

avoid – *vermeiden*, **begin**[1] – *anfangen*, **carry on** – *weitermachen*, **consider** – *sich überlegen*, **continue**[1] – *fortfahren*, **dislike** – *nicht mögen*, **enjoy** – *gern tun*, **finish** – *fertig werden*, **give up** – *aufgeben*, **go on** – *weitermachen*, **hate** – *hassen*, **imagine** – sich *vorstellen*, **intend** – *beabsichtigen*, **like** – *mögen*, **love** – *lieben*, **mind** – *etwas einzuwenden haben gegen*, **miss** – *vermissen*, **quit** – *aufhören*, **practise** – *üben*, **prefer** – *vorziehen*, **risk** – *riskieren*, **start**[1] – *anfangen*, **stop** – *aufhören*, **suggest** – *vorschlagen*

[1]Diese Verben kann man ohne Bedeutungsunterschied auch mit dem Infinitiv verwenden.

➤ Verben + Infinitiv

afford – *sich leisten*, **choose** – *wählen*, **consider** – *halten für*, **decide** – *entscheiden*, **expect** – *erwarten*, **hope** – *hoffen*, **manage** – *es schaffen, etwas zu tun*, **offer** – *anbieten*, **promise** – *versprechen*, **refuse** – *sich weigern*, **seem** – *scheinen*, **wish** – *wünschen*

➤ Ausdrücke + -ing

it's (no) **fun**, **there's no sense in**, **it's** (not) **worth**
Übrigens: Benutze kein Passiv nach **worth**:
L.A. is **worth** visiting. Nicht: ~~L.A. is worth being visited.~~

Exam Tip 24 Nach ***like, love, hate, prefer*** unterscheidet man heutzutage kaum noch zwischen Infinitiv und Gerundium. In der Praxis sind sie austauschbar, da der Unterschied so geringfügig ist. Richte dich nach dem im Unterricht gebrauchten Lehrwerk. Vergiss nicht, dass man ***would like / love / hate / prefer*** immer mit dem Infinitiv benutzt!

Exercise 1 Richtig oder falsch? Bessere jeden falschen Satz entsprechend aus.

1 I intend to make a film with the Danish star, Emil Hye-Knudsen.

____

____

2 His films are certainly worth being watched – some people consider him being a genius *[Genie]* and everybody expects him to win an Oscar.

____

____

3 There's no sense to carry on to study French much longer if you dislike to learn foreign languages.

____

____

4 I hate having to talk in front of lots of people – I'd prefer avoiding situations like that.

____

____

5 Paul is considering to look for a new job. If the company refuses to give him more money, he'll probably stop to work for them.

____

____

6 Would you mind to close the window, please?

____

7 If we manage making a profit again, people will continue to invest *[investieren]*.

____

____

➤ **Merke dir auch folgende feststehende -ing-Kombinationen:**

Adjektiv + Präposition + -ing:
afraid of, bad at, fed up (with), good at, proud of, sick of, tired of, used to

Substantiv + Präposition + -ing:
chance of, danger of, difficulty in, possibility of, reason for, trouble in

Verb + Präposition + -ing:
believe in, consist of, decide against, depend on, dream of, insist on, succeed in, think of

Außerdem
feel like, look forward to

Exercise 2 Vervollständige folgende Sätze mit einer Präposition und -ing.

1 Brian has decided ________________ to Cornwall at Easter. ↝ *travel*

2 Is there any possibility ________ the Conservatives ____________ the election? ↝ *win*

3 The Conservatives can't depend ____________________ ____________ a majority this time. ↝ *get*

4 Brian is proud ________________ a Scot. ↝ *be*

5 I'm fed ________________ to make her understand. Perhaps I'm just no good ________________ things. ↝ *try, explain*

6 You'll never succeed ________________ the top because you're not used ________________ hard. ↝ *reach, work*

7 He dreams ________________ a pop star, but he has no chance ____________ so. ↝ *become, do*

➤ Verben mit -ing oder Infinitv, bei denen es einen Bedeutungsunterschied gibt.

remember to do sth. – *daran denken, etwas zu tun*
remember doing sth. – *sich erinnern, etwas getan zu haben*

forget to do sth. – *vergessen, etwas zu tun*
forget doing sth. – *vergessen, etwas getan zu haben*

stop to do – *anhalten, um etwas (anderes) zu tun*
stop doing sth. – *aufhören, etwas zu tun*

Exercise 3 Übersetze die fehlenden, pinkfarbenen Satzteile und benutze dabei Gerundium oder Infinitiv mit: remember (2x), forget (2x), stop (2x).

1 *Vergiss bitte nicht, ihn bei der Arbeit anzurufen.* ______________________

____

____

at work.

2 *Hör auf, die ganze Zeit so viel Unsinn zu reden!* ________________

____

______________________ the whole time.

3 *Ich werde nie vergessen, wie ich zum ersten Mal nach Brasilien flog.* ____

____________________ to Brazil for the first time.

4 *Uli konnte nicht aufhören, über seine eigenen Witze zu lachen.*

____

______________________ at his jokes.

5 *Denke daran, ihn sofort zu informieren.* ______________________

____ .

6 *Jedermann erinnert sich, wie Becker das Spiel in Wimbeldon verlor.* ______________________________________ Becker

__________________________________ the game in Wimbeldon.

B 10 Adjektiv oder Adverb?

Streiche jeden Satz, in dem du einen Fehler findest.

1.1 The question was very simple and she answered him quickly
1.2 The question was very simply and she answered him quick.
1.3 Can you give me a quick answer, please.

2.1 She easily solved the problem.
2.2 She solved easy the problem.
2.3 She easyly solved the problem.

3.1 The table was arranged beautifully.
3.2 The table was arranged beautiful.

4.1 They ate hungry the pizza.
4.2 They hungrily ate the pizza.
4.3 They ate hungrily the pizza.
4.4 They ate the pizza hungrily.

5.1 He's exhausted because he worked very hard to finish the job.
5.2 He's exhausted because he hardly worked to finish the job.

6.1 It's a high intelligent animal.
6.2 It's a highly intelligent animal.
6.3 It's a highly intelligently animal.

7.1 She smiled at him friendly.
7.2 She gave him a lovely pair of boxer shorts.

8.1 He didn't repair my bike very well.
8.2 His brother wasn't very good, either.

9.1 He lives quite near the school. You can walk there
9.2 He lives nearly the school. You can walk there.
9.3 The weather was so nice that I nearly walked.

10.1 Luckily, he can speak Japanese.
10.2 Lucky, he can speak Japanese.

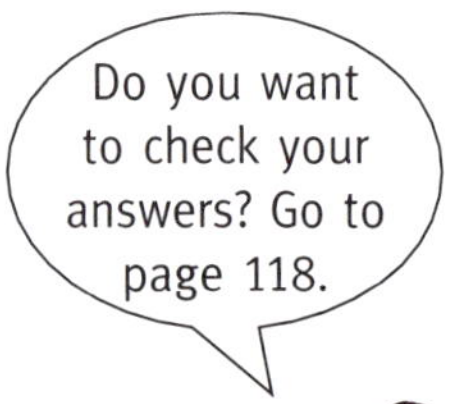

Hast du das gekonnt?
Falls du nicht alle falschen Sätze identifiziert hast, mache weiter mit diesem Abschnitt (Seite 69).
Falls du die Aufgabe richtig lösen konntest, mache weiter mit dem nächsten Abschnitt (Seite 71).

- Im Englischen unterscheiden sich in der Regel die Formen von Adjektiven (Eigenschaftswörter), die Hauptwörter beschreiben, und Adverben (Umstandswörter), die meistens Tätigkeitswörter, aber auch Eigenschaftswörter, andere Umstandswörter oder ganze Sätze beschreiben. Alle fettgedruckten Wörter im folgenden Satz sind Adverben und alle schräggestellten Wörter sind Adjektive:

  Unfortunately, John is not **very** *intelligent* and **usually** works **rather slowly** at his *old* computer.

  Die **regelmäßigen** Adverben werden durch Anhängen der Endung -ly an das Adjektiv gebildet. Die Schreibweise ändert sich je nach Endung des Adjektivs. Beachte:

  quick → quickly **beautiful → beautifully** **full → fully**
  true → truly **simple → simply**
  basic → basically **busy → busily**

  - Allerdings gibt es **Abweichungen** von den Umbildungsregeln oben. Es bleibt nichts anderes übrig als folgende Einzelfälle zu lernen:
    shy → shyly, **public → publicly**,
    friendly, **silly**, **lovely → in a friendly / silly / lovely way**

  - Folgende Wörter haben **dieselbe Form** als Adjektiv oder Adverb:
    early, **extra**, **fast**, **little**, **long**, **low**, **straight**, **weekly**, **monthly**, **yearly**, **daily**

- Auch folgende Wörter haben **dieselbe Form** als Adjektiv und Adverb, allerdings gibt es bei jedem eine -ly-Version, die eine ganz **andere Bedeutung** hat:

  hard – *schwer, hart* → **hardly** – *kaum*
  free – *umsonst* → **freely** – *offen, freimütig*
  high – *hoch hinauf* → **highly** – *hoch, höchst*
  late – *zu spät* → **lately** – *in letzter Zeit, neulich*
  most – *am meisten* → **mostly** – *meistens*
  near – *nahe heran* → **nearly** – *fast, beinahe*
  pretty – *ziemlich, hübsch* → **prettily** – *hübsch*

- Und dieses wichtige Wort hat sogar zwei total **verschiedene Formen**:
  Adjektiv: **good** → Adverb: **well**

- Näheres über die **Satzstellung** von Adverben findet ihr in B11 – Seite 71 ff.

······· **Exam Tip 25** Ein Adverb steht nie zwischen Verb und Objekt!

Exercise Unterstreiche jeweils das richtige Wort.

1 The alarm clock rang very *early* / *earlily*, and Jane turned it off *quick* / *quickly*, then *slow* / *slowly* got out of bed.

2 Her back was still *painful* / *painfully* after all that *difficult* / *with great difficulty* work yesterday.

3 Tom had worked *quite* / *quietly*, *hard* / *hardly* too, but he never managed to do things *very good* / *very well*.

4 However, they had decorated the hall *beautiful* / *beautifully*, and their *year* / *yearly* party would be *fantastic* / *fantastically*, she was sure.

5 *Sudden / Suddenly* she remembered those *terrible* / *terribly* flowers.

6 The ones they wanted for the tables were *unfortunate* / *unfortunately* much too *expensive* / *expensively* in the shop, so she planned to take some from her mother's garden *secret* / *secretly*.

7 Jane's mother was very *nice* / *nicely*, but not very *generous* / *generously* with her *pretty* / *prettily* flowers.

8 Jane dressed *quick* / *quickly*, then walked *quiet* / *quietly* down the stairs, and into the garden, closing the door very *carefuly* / *carefully* behind her, so that her parents wouldn't wake up.

B 11 Die Steigerung von Adjektiven und Adverben

Streiche jeden Satz, in dem du einen Fehler findest.

1.1 That's the simplest solution.
1.2 That's the most simple solution.

2.1 Tillie and Meg are both clever, but I think Meg is cleverer.
2.2 Tillie and Meg are both clever, but I think Meg is more clever.

3.1 Take that chair. It's comfortabler.
3.2 Take that chair. It's more comfortable.

4.1 I think you'd be more happy here.
4.2 I think you'd be happier here.

5.1 That radio is the most expensive of these models.
5.2 That radio is most expensive of these models.
5.3 That radio is expensivest of these models.

6.1 Don't ask Bill. John usually works harder like Bill.
6.2 Don't ask Bill. John usually works harder than Bill.
6.3 Don't ask Bill. John usually works harder as Bill.

7.1 She isn't so intelligent like her sister.
7.2 She isn't as intelligent as her sister.
7.3 She isn't so intelligent as her sister.

8.1 Your car is very much like mine.
8.2 Your car is very much as mine.

9.1 He painted his second picture more badly than the first.
9.2 He painted his second picture more badly as the first.
9.3 He painted his second picture worse as the first.
9.4 He painted his second picture worse than the first.

Hast du das gekonnt?
Falls du nicht alle falschen Sätze identifiziert hast, mache weiter mit diesem Abschnitt (Seite 72).
Falls du die Aufgabe richtig lösen konntest, mache weiter mit dem nächsten Abschnitt (Seite 74).

➤ Im Englischen gibt es für **Adjektive zwei Arten der Steigerung**.

Bei der Steigerung mit **-er** (1. Steigerungsstufe) und **-est** (2. Steigerungsstufe) werden beide an das Adjektiv einfach angehängt. Diese Art Steigerung wird benutzt bei **einsilbigen** Wörtern:

sweet → **sweeter** → **sweetest**
nice → **nicer** → **nicest**
big → **bigger** → **biggest**

bei **zweisilbigen** Wörtern die auf -le enden:
simple → **simpler** → **simplest**

und bei **zweisilbigen** Wörtern die auf -y enden:
happy → **happier** → **happiest**

Beachte die veränderte Schreibweise bei den Steigerungen oben.

Mit **more** (1. Steigerungsstufe) und **most** (2. Steigerungsstufe) werden alle anderen zweisilbigen Adjektive, und alle die drei oder mehr Silben haben, gesteigert:
more modern, **(the) most** stupid, **more** excited, **(the) most** beautiful

➤ **Adverben** werden in der Regel mit **more** oder **most** **gesteigert:**
more easily, **more** brilliantly

Wenn die **Form** von Adverb und Adjektiv gleich ist, wird wie bei Adjektiven gesteigert:
He drives **more** carefully **than me,** but **much** faster.

Beachte folgende **unregelmäßige** Steigerungsformen:
good / **well** → **better** → **best**
bad / **badly** → **worse** → **worst**
far → **further** → **furthest**

➤ Und so stellt man **Vergleiche** im Englischen an:
It's / It isn't **as** easy **as** I thought. – *Es ist (nicht) so leicht wie ich dachte.*
She is **like** her mother. – *Sie ist wie ihre Mutter.*
He lives furth**er** from town **than** me. –
Er wohnt weiter von der Stadt entfernt als ich.
But you can get there **more** easily. –
Aber du kannst dort leichter hinkommen.
It's **the most** expensive radio **of** all. –
Es ist das teuerste Radio von allen.

dir die
ungsanzeigen
ıd ergänze die
:. Benutze dabei
ichtige
erung der
gebenen Wörter.

near center, $650 / month

House with big yard, 5 rooms, 15 miles from city center, $450 / month

1 room studio, near university, 5 miles from center, $125 / month

Luxury apartment, 3 rooms plus terrace, in center, $550 / month

Of these three homes, the house is ______________________ from the city center. → *far*

2 I think a house with a big yard is ______________________ an apartment for a family with children. → *good*

3 The studio apartment would be ______________________ place of these three homes for a student, but ______________ ________ place for a family of five people. → *good / bad*

4 The home for $550 isn't ______________________ the home for $450. → *large*

5 The 3-room apartment is ______________________ the house, but perhaps it's ______________________ to take care of. → *expensive / easy*

6 Do you think the luxury apartment would be ______________________________ the house? → *comfortable*

7 I'd like the house, because it's ______________ and probably ______________________ of all three. → *big / quiet*

8 The house in this picture is ____________ _____ I've ever seen. It's much ____________ ______________________ my sister's. → *lovely / interesting*

B 12 Mit oder ohne Artikel?

Streiche jeden Satz, in dem du einen Fehler findest.

1.1 The lunch is usually the only time I eat the soup.
1.2 The lunch is usually the only time I eat soup.
1.3 Lunch is usually the only time I eat soup.

2.1 I live in the West End close to the Oxford Street.
2.2 I live in the West End close to Oxford Street.
2.3 I live in West End close to the Oxford Street.

3.1 Tea is better than coffee for breakfast.
3.2 The tea is better than the coffee for breakfast.
3.3 Tea is better than coffee for the breakfast.
3.4 The tea is better than coffee for the breakfast.

4.1 Death is simply a part of the life.
4.2 The death is simply a part of life.
4.3 Death is simply a part of life.

5.1 Jutta works as doctor in the Philippines.
5.2 Jutta works as a doctor in the Philippines.

6.1 As admirer *[Bewunderer]* of Gandhi, Marc is against the violence.
6.2 As admirer of Gandhi, Marc is against violence.
6.3 As an admirer of Gandhi, Marc is against violence.

7.1 Who once said: "War is the hell."?
7.2 Who once said: "War is hell."?

8.1 Not many people go to the church on the Sunday.
8.2 Not many people go to church on Sunday.
8.3 Not many people go to the church on Sunday.

Hast du das gekonnt?
Falls du nicht alle falschen Sätze identifiziert hast, mache weiter mit diesem Abschnitt (Seite 75).
Falls du die Aufgabe richtig lösen konntest, mache weiter mit dem nächsten Abschnitt (Seite 79).

Exam Tip 26 *all the ...* bedeutet **alle** aus einer bestimmten Anzahl, z.B. *All the teachers in this school are crazy.* Meint man *all* ganz allgemein, benutzt man kein *the*.

- Bei **the** / **a(n)** prägt man sich am besten möglichst viele typische Zusammenhänge ein, denn der Gebrauch ist anders als im Deutschen. Besonders Ortsnamen wie **the** Bronx, **the** Empire State Building, **the** Tower (of London) muss man auswendig lernen.

- **Der bestimmte Artikel: the**

Ohne Artikel stehen
Abstrakta wie **hate**, **life**, **love**, ... im allgemeinen Sinne;
Stoffnamen wie **bread**, **oil**, ... z.B. **Oil** is used for heating.
Mahlzeiten wie **breakfast**, **lunch**, ...

Aber: Wenn etwas näher bestimmt wird:
The life of people in India is often hard. (of-Ergänzung)
The oil that Saudi Arabia produces is cheap. (Relativsatz)

Ohne Artikel stehen
Wochentage wie **on Tuesday**, ...
Monate wie **in May**, ...
die meisten **Straßen**- und **Bergnamen** wie **Wall Street**, **Oxford Street**, **Ben Nevis**, **Mount Fuji**, ...
Eigennamen wie **good old Sarah**, **King Charles**, **Uncle Harry**, ...

Aber: the Alps, **the Rockies**, **the Strand** (Londoner Straße)

Ohne Artikel stehen
church, **hospital**, **prison**, **school**, **university**, wenn es um den **Zweck des Gebäudes** geht, d.h. bei **hospital** – *ärztliche Behandlung.*
Wenn es aber um das **Gebäude selbst** geht, steht der Artikel, z.B.
A man was sent to **prison** for shoplifting. Afterwards he felt really sorry and gave his money to **the church** in his village.

- **Der unbestimmte Artikel: a(n)**

Mit Artikel stehen
Berufe, politische Parteien, normalerweise auch **Konfessionen** wie **Jew**, **Catholic** und **Nationalitäten** wie **Frenchman**, **Scotsman**, ...
z.B. She's **a lawyer** and **a Conservative**.

Der Artikel wird außerdem
nach **as** verwendet, z.B. She did it **as a** joke.

Exam Tip 27 Vorsicht bei Zahlen:
hundert – ***a*** / ***one*** *hundred;*
tausend – ***a*** / ***one*** *thousand;*
hundert Leute – ***a*** / ***one*** *hundred people.*

Exercise 1 Richtig oder falsch? Streiche in den folgenden Sätzen die falschen Artikel durch oder setze den richtigen Artikel ein.

1 He lives somewhere in *East End* of London.

___

2 *The Aunt Mary* wants to study at *the university*.

___

3 They painted some rooms in *school* in *the June*.

___

4 *The St Paul's Cathedral* is situated in *the City* and is not far from *the Tower of London* or *Strand*. ___

___

5 *The White House* in *USA* is the home of the President – just like *the 10 Downing Street* in *the UK*. ___

___

6 *As girl* I grew up in *the Bronx* – my parents came from *the Switzerland* after *the World War II* (my father was *Jew* and worked *as subway driver* in the city). ___

___

___

7 *Poor Peter* died *on Monday* just *before dinner*.

___

8 *The violence of tomorrow* will be a product of *the society of today*.

___

9 Everybody eats *the bread*, and *bread* that they bake here in Germany is wonderful. ___

___

10 I've climbed *Ben Nevis* but not *the Mount Everest.*

____

11 These ones cost *hundred dollars* each.

____

12 *Uncle Jan* is *Dutchman* and lives in *Netherlands.*

____

13 *The Queen Victoria* once said: "We are not amused!"

____

➤ **Feste Wendungen mit und ohne the**

mit: most of **the** time, on **the** phone, on **the** radio
Man kann sowohl on television als auch on **the** television sagen.

ohne: most people, in case, in bed, in public, at work, by bike / bus / car / plane / ship, play the guitar

➤ **Feste Wendungen mit und ohne a(n)**

mit: be in **a** position (to do sth.) – *in der Lage sein (etwas zu tun)*

in **a** loud voice – *mit lauter Stimme*
in **a** hurry – *in Eile*
in **a** friendly way – *auf freundliche Art*
as **a** rule – *in der Regel*
for **a** change – *zur Abwechslung*
without **a** break – *ohne Pause / Unterbrechung*
have **a** headache / temperature – *Kopfweh / Fieber haben*
take **an** interest in – *Interesse haben an*
take **a** seat – *Platz nehmen*
make **a** noise – *Lärm machen*
smoke **a** pipe – *Pfeife rauchen*
half **an** hour – *eine halbe Stunde*
$150 **a** day / month / … – *$150 am Tag / im Monat / …*
What **a** pity! – *Wie schade!*

ohne: What nonsense! – *Was für ein Unsinn!*
What lovely weather! – *Was für ein schönes Wetter!*
Die letzten zwei Wendungen stehen im Englischen immer **ohne a**!

Exercise 2 Übersetze jeweils den farbigen Satzteil mit einer passenden Wendung von Seite 77.

1 *Er spricht immer mit lauter Stimme.*

He always speaks ______________________________ .

2 *Annie verdient tausend Dollar im Monat.*

Annie earns ______________________________ .

3 *In der Regel rauche ich Pfeife.*

______________________________ .

4 *Sie soll mich anrufen, falls sie schon bei der Arbeit ist.*

She should call me __________ she's already ______________ .

5 *Die meiste Zeit liegt er im Bett am Telefon.*

______________ he's lying ______________________ .

6 *Ich bin in Eile und habe nur einen halben Tag in Tokyo.*

______________________ and have only ____________________

in Tokyo.

7 *Wie schade, dass du mich nicht im Fernsehen gesehen hast.*

____________________ that you didn't see me ____________ .

8 *Aber ich hörte dein Lied im Radio.*

But I heard your song ______________________________ .

9 *Die meisten Leute hatten Kopfweh bei dem vielen Rauch im Zimmer.* ______________________________ with all that smoke in the room.

10 *Vor langer Zeit spielte er Gitarre und Klavier.*

A long time ago ______________________________

______________ .

11 *Am Mittwoch arbeitete sie ohne Unterbrechung.*

______________ she worked ______________________ .

12 *„Was für ein Unsinn!" schrie er.*

"____________________________ !" he shouted.

B 13 Zählbare oder nicht zählbare Substantive

Streiche jeden Satz, in dem du einen Fehler findest.

1.1 There isn't many time to do this test.
1.2 We haven't got a lot of time left.
1.3 The prisoner didn't have much time with his girlfriend.

2.1 How many times have I told you not to kiss that turtle?
2.2 She's been to that restaurant a lot of times.
2.3 We've tried to call him very much times.

3.1 There aren't many money in my wallet.
3.2 We haven't got much eggs
3.3 We've got a lot of butter, but not many nuts.

4.1 There is a lot of water on the bathroom floor.
4.2 There is many water on the bathroom floor.
4.3 There is much water on the bathroom floor.

5.1 I think there are a few flowers left in the garden.
5.2 We've finally had a little warm weather the past few days.
5.3 Can you put a few more ater in that vase.

Could you bring me some oranges, please?

6.1 I'd love to, but I'm afraid there are really very few in this bowl.
6.2 I'd love to, but I'm afraid there are really a very few in this bowl.
6.3 I'd love to, but I'm afraid there is really little in this bowl.
6.4 I'd love to, but I'm afraid there is really the least in this bowl.

7.1 Don't worry! There are quite a few oranges in the cellar.
7.2 Don't worry! There are quite a little oranges in the cellar.
7.3 Don't worry! There are quite a lot of oranges in the cellar.
7.4 Don't worry! There are very few oranges in the cellar.

8.1 There are fewer people for volleyball and too many for rummy.
8.2 There are less people for volleyball and too much for rummy.

9.1 She has the most time but the least money.
9.2 She has the more time but the fewer money.

Hast du das gekonnt?

Falls du nicht alle falschen Sätze identifiziert hast,
mache weiter mit diesem Abschnitt (Seite 80).
Falls du die Aufgabe richtig lösen konntest,
mache weiter mit dem nächsten Abschnitt (Seite 83).

➤ Wenn man in Englischen eine allgemeine Mengenbestimmung vor ein Substantiv (Hauptwort) setzt, muss man erst entscheiden, ob es sich um ein **zählbares** oder ein **nicht zählbares** Substantiv handelt. Das heißt, ob es einen Sinn ergibt, wenn man eine Zahl davor setzt und ob man einen Plural (Mehrzahl) von diesem Wort bilden kann. Wenn ja, ist es ein zählbares Substantiv.
Zählbar: apple, five apples, dollar, fifty dollars
Nicht zählbar: milk, butter, noise, money

➤ Beachte, dass einige Wörter mit verschiedener Bedeutung zählbar oder nicht zählbar sein können. Ein sehr wichtiges Beispiel:
time → He called me three **times**. – *mal*
time → I haven't got much time tomorrow morning. – *Zeit*

Vergiss auch nicht die Wörter, die im Deutschen Plural sind und im Englischen Singular wie: **information**, **furniture**, … (vgl. A1, Seite 9). Wenn der Unterschied zwischen zählbar und nicht zählbar klar ist, kannst du die passende Mengenbestimmung wie folgt zuordnen.

Zählbar	**Nicht zählbar**
a, **an**, **some**, **any** – *ein, eine, einige* **not any** – *keine* Here's **a** banana and **an** orange. There are **some** brown shoes, but there aren't **any** red ones.	**some**, **any** – *etwas, einige* **not any**– *keine* There is **some** juice in that jug. We haven't got **any** information.
a lot of – *viel* vorwiegend in bejahenden Sätzen There are **a lot of** soldiers here.	**a lot of** – *viel* vorwiegend in bejahenden Sätzen I think there is **a lot of** trouble.
many – *viel* in Fragen und Verneinungen und mit **too** Are there **many** students in your class? You've got **too many** onions in the salad.	**much** – *viel* in Fragen und Verneinungen und mit **too** There isn't **much** money in the bank. This city has **too much** pollution.
few, **a few** – *wenige, ein wenig, ein paar* There are **few** parks, but there are **a few** good beaches.	**little**, **a little** – *wenig, ein wenig* There is **little** time left, but we've still got **a little** energy.

··· Exam Tip 28 ***quite a few*** – ziemlich viel (häufig gebraucht)
*We've got **quite a few** doctors in our street.*
quite a little – ziemlich viel (selten gebraucht)
*There's **quite a little** crime in Miami.*

➤ Beachte, dass die Mengenbestimmungen auf Seite 80 auch ohne Substantiv stehen können, aber man trotzdem entscheiden muss, ob sie **zählbare** oder **nicht zählbare** Substantive ersetzen.
Have they got any camels in that zoo?
Well, not **many**, but I think there are **a few**.

Exercise 1 Setze die richtigen Mengenbestimmungen ein.

Dear Boris, Glasgow, 3rd April ...

When I look at the date on this letter, I can't believe ______________ ↝ so viel ↝ time has passed since we moved to Glasgow. I really like it here. I have ______________ ↝ ein paar ↝ good friends and there are really ______________ ↝ viele ↝ fun things to do. The best thing about this place is the beach. Last weekend ______________ ↝ einige ↝ friends and I packed ______________ ↝ ein paar ↝ sandwiches, ______________ ↝ ein wenig ↝ fruit and ______________ ↝ viele ↝ cold drinks and went to our favourite spot. Of course, we had ______________ ↝ zu wenig ↝ food with us, and there was ______________ ↝ ziemlich viel ↝ wind, but we had ______________ ↝ viel ↝ fun! When you come to visit me next summer, we'll go on ______________ ↝ viele ↝ beach picnics. But I should warn you, that there are ______________ ↝ sehr wenig ↝ places near here where you can go diving, and also ______________ ↝ sehr wenig ↝ surfing. How is school this year? Are there ______________ ↝ viele ↝ new students? Have you got ______________ ↝ viel ↝ homework? It's hard to believe, but there are a lot of weekends when I ______________ ↝ haben / keine ↝.

- ➤ **A lot of, many** und **much** werden alle mit **more** (1. Steigerungsstufe) und **(the) most** (2. Steigerungsstufe) gesteigert.
- ➤ **Few** wird mit **fewer** (1. Steigerungsstufe), **(the) fewest** (2. Steigerungsstufe) gesteigert.
- ➤ **Little** wird mit **less** (1. Steigerungsstufe), **(the) least** (2. Steigerungsstufe) gesteigert.

Exercise 2 Here's a picture of the beach near the town center.

Of course, there are ____________________ *am meisten* people at this particular beach at the weekend, when the weather's good. But you only have to walk __________________ *ein paar mehr* kilometers away from the centre, and you can find __________________ *viel mehr* wonderful spots where there are __________________ *weniger* swimmers and ___________________ *weniger* noise. The water in the sea here has ____________________________ *am wenigsten* pollution on the whole coast. Unfortunately, it also has __________________________ *am wenigsten* lobsters. You have to go further north for them.

B 14 Zusammensetzungen mit some, any, every

Streiche jeden Satz, in dem du einen Fehler findest.

1.1 There's someone here to see you.
1.2 There's anyone here to see you.

2.1 Would you like something to drink. We've got coke or coffee.
2.2 Would you like anything to drink? We've got coke or coffee.

3.1 Have you got anything to eat?
3.2 Have you got something to eat?

4.1 My basket isn't anywhere in this room.
4.2 My basket isn't somewhere in the room.

5.1 I've done everything I can for them. I can't do any more.
5.2 I've done anything I can for them. I can't do any more.

6.1 Everybody here is hungry. We need 20 hamburgers.
6.2 Everybody here are hungry. We need 20 hamburgers.
6.3 All here are hungry. We need 20 hamburgers.

7.1 Sorry. We haven't got anything for a headache.
7.2 Sorry. We haven't got something for a headache.
7.3 Sorry. We've got nothing for a headache.

The key for this test is on page 119.

8.1 Look at this room.
Everything is a mess.
8.2 Look at this room.
Everything are a mess.
8.3 Look at this room.
All is a mess.

9.1 I'll do anything you say.
9.2 I'll do something you say.

Hast du das gekonnt?
Falls du nicht alle falschen Sätze identifiziert hast, mache weiter mit diesem Abschnitt (Seite 84).
Falls du die Aufgabe richtig lösen konntest, mache weiter mit dem nächsten Abschnitt (Seite 86).

➤ Die Ableitungen von **some** benutzt man grundsätzlich in bejahenden Sätzen, sowie in Fragen, die sich auf vorhandene Dinge beziehen, wie bei Angeboten und Bitten.
We've got **somebody** here who can cook for us.
Would you like **something** to drink? We've got **some** milk and juice.

➤ Die Ableitungen von **any** werden grundsätzlich in verneinenden Sätzen benutzt sowie in Fragen, bei denen die Existenz von etwas in Frage gestellt wird.
Oh dear. I haven't got **anything** to eat. Have you got **anything**?
Is there **anybody** here who can change a 5-pound note?

➤ **Any** und die Ableitungen davon treten nur dann in bejahenden Sätzen auf, wenn sie die Bedeutung *irgendein / jedes beliebige / egal welches / alle* haben.
You can call me **any** time. I would do **anything** to help you.

➤ Beachte: **Nobody** / **No one** kann **not anybody** ersetzen,
wie **nothing** → **not anything**,
und **nowhere** → **not anywhere** ersetzen kann.

Exercise 1 Ergänze den Brief mit den folgenden Wörtern

anyone • any • some • anything • something • someone • anywhere

I really want to give Dad ______________ special for his 50th birthday, but I just can't think of ______________ . Do you know if ______________ is giving him a pipe? He hasn't had ______________ new ones for a long time, and I could buy him a nice one with ______________ of his favourite tobacco. Is there ______________ in town where they sell Cumberland Mix, that blend he used to buy in Manchester? If I can't find it, I'll give him ______________ for his garden work. You know that he likes ______________ connected with gardening, regardless of what it is. But what can I afford? Have you got ______________ ideas? I'll appreciate ______________ help you can give me.

➤ **Jeder**, sowie **alle** oder **alles** als Substantive, werden nie mit **all** übersetzt, sondern mit **everybody** oder **everything**.
Als Mengenbestimmung kann man **all** zusammen mit **of the** verwenden:
Everybody came to the party. **All of the students** were very glad.

➤ Bei **every** und den Zusammensetzungen von every wie **everyone**, **everything**, **everywhere** folgt das Verb jeweils im Singular.
Everything is all right. **Everybody is** going to help.

Exercise 2 Ergänze die Sätze mit der Übersetzung der angegebenen Wörter.

I've asked ____________ *alle* to look after my tropical fish over the holidays, but I'm afraid ____________ *niemand* can do it. So far ____________ *jeder* has had a different excuse, and a good one. I would hate to lose the fish. ____________ *alle sagen* you can't get fish like those ____________ *überall* these days. Now you're my last hope.

____________ *sind alle* in your family away over the holidays? I would be very grateful if one of you, or ____________ *ihr alle* could help me. Don't worry about buying food. ____________ *alles ist* in the bag that I would bring with them. Just give them a little every day. And you don't need to clean their tank. Let me know if you can help!

B 15 Bestimmende oder nicht bestimmende Relativsätze

Streiche jeden Satz, in dem du einen Fehler findest.

1.1 People who live in glass houses shouldn't throw stones.
1.2 People, who live in glass houses, shouldn't throw stones.
1.3 People whom live in glass houses shouldn't throw stones.

2.1 The woman who I met at our school was from Brampton College.
2.2 The woman that I met at our school was from Brampton College.
2.3 The woman where I met at our school was from Brampton College.
2.4 The woman, who I met at our school, was from Brampton College.

3.1 There are a lot of things that I don't like here.
3.2 There are a lot of things which I don't like here.
3.3 There are a lot of things, what I don't like here.

4.1 The student, who she is talking to, is my brother.
4.2 The student to whom she is talking is my brother.
4.3 The student who she is talking to is my brother.
4.4 The student which she is talking to is my brother.

5.1 A stadium is a place in which you can watch sports events.
5.2 A stadium is a place where you can watch sports events.
5.3 A stadium is a place what you can watch sports events.

6.1 Our house, which we bought in 1975, has always been a problem.
6.2 Our house that we bought in 1975 has always been a problem.
6.3 Our house, what we bought in 1975, has always been a problem.
6.4 Our house which we bought in 1975 has always been a problem.

7.1 Dylan Thomas, that wrote Under Milkwood, was from Wales.
7.2 Dylan Thomas who wrote Under Milkwood was from Wales.
7.3 Dylan Thomas, who wrote Under Milkwood, was from Wales.

8.1 She doesn't like vegetables, which makes it very difficult to cook for her.
8.2 She doesn't like vegetables, what makes it very difficult to cook for her.
8.3 She doesn't like vegetables, that makes it very difficult to cook for her.

Hast du das gekonnt?
Falls du nicht alle falschen Sätze identifiziert hast, mache weiter mit diesen Abschnitt (Seite 87).

Falls du die Aufgabe richtig lösen konntest, mache weiter mit dem nächsten Abschnitt (Seite 90).

➤ **Bestimmende Relativsätze**

Relativsätze sind Nebensätze, die ein Substantiv im Hauptsatz näher definieren. Wenn diese Definition für das Verständnis des Satzes notwendig ist, handelt es sich um einen notwendigen oder bestimmenden Relativsatz. Wenn der bestimmende Relativsatz sich auf eine Person bezieht, kann er von **who** / **that**, **whom**, **whose** (dessen, deren) eingeleitet werden:
The people **who (that) took the photographs** are here.
They're the ones **whose car was stolen.**
He's the man t**o whom she is talking.** (He's the man **who she's talking to**.)

➤ Wenn sich der notwendige Relativsatz auf Sachen bezieht, wird er von **which** oder **that** eingeleitet:
It's something **which (that) you use to clean your car with.**

➤ Nach Substantiven, die einen Ort bezeichnen, kann ein Relativsatz auch mit **where** anfangen:
A box office is a place **where you buy theatre tickets.**
Wenn das Substantiv eine Zeit bezeichnet, auch mit **when**:
Summer is the season **when I feel best.**

➤ Niemals Kommas, Klammern oder Gedankenstriche in bestimmenden Relativsätzen.

➤ **Nicht bestimmende Relativsätze**

Wenn ein Relativsatz nur zusätzliche Information über den Hauptsatz gibt und nicht wichtig ist, um den Satz sinnvoll zu machen, handelt es sich um einen nicht bestimmenden Relativsatz. Hier ist **that** keine Alternative zu **who** oder **which**:
Tom Switchworth, **who arrived early this morning**, is staying in Room 23.

➤ **Which** kann sich auch auf den ganzen Hauptsatz beziehen:
He's looking after the children this evening, **which makes it very difficult for him to come to the meeting**.

➤ Immer Kommas, Klammern oder Gedankenstriche in nicht bestimmenden Relativsätzen.

···· **Exam Tip 29** *What* kommt nie in einem Relativsatz vor!

Exercise 1 Ergänze die Sätze. Verbinde jeweils den zweiten Satz als bestimmenden oder nicht bestimmenden Relativsatz mit dem Hauptsatz. Benutze **who**, **whom**, **which**, **where**, oder **when**. Vergiss nicht Kommas einzusetzen, wo es notwendig ist.

1 Here's a picture of the Japanese exchange teacher ______________

____ .

He taught music at our school last year.

2 Mr Nagasaki didn't speak very good English ______________

____ .

It made things a bit difficult.

3 The Four Seasons ______________________________

______________________ was his favourite piece of music.

It was composed by Antonio Vivaldi.

4 A Japanese composer wrote a piece ______________________

____ .

It is very similar to Vivaldi's Four Seasons.

5 This piece ______________________________________

______________ was performed by our school orchestra last year.

It is called the Japanese Four Seasons.

6 *The man* ______________________________________

______________ *is our present music teacher.*

My father is talking to him.

7 He is the one ____

____ .

He spent a year at Mr Nagasaki's school in Japan.

8 I think Kyoto was the place ______________________ .

He lived there.

9 Ms Clarington ____

______________________ took all of these pictures.

She organizes the teacher exchange programmes.

10 Unfortunately the pictures

____

____

didn't turn out. I took them at the concert.

11 I took them at a time _____

____

____

______________________ .

My camera wasn't working very well.

Exercise 2 Schreibe die Sätze auf, bei denen man auch **that** verwenden kann.

____

____

____

____

____

____

B 16 If-Sätze

Streiche jeden Satz, in dem du einen Fehler findest.

1.1 If he would say that to me, I would be annoyed.
1.2 If he says that to me, I had been annoyed.
1.3 If he had said that to me, I had been annoyed.
1.4 If he said that to me, I would be annoyed.

2.1 We would have moved to London if we got married.
2.2 We will move to London if we will get married.
2.3 We will move to London if we get married.
2.4 We had moved to London if we had got married.

3.1 If I'll go to Britain, I must visit Kent.
3.2 If I go to Britain, I must visit Kent.
3.3 If I go to Britain, I must have visited Kent.

4.1 He would have helped them if they would ask him.
4.2 He would have helped them if they'd asked him.
4.3 He would have helped them if they'll ask him.
4.4 He had helped them if they would ask him.

5.1 I would love to meet the Queen if I were invited.
5.2 I've loved to meet the Quuen if I'm invited.
5.3 I'll love to meet the Queen if I'm invited.
5.4 I would love to meet her if I would be invited.

6.1 She's not prepared to help unless we pay her.
6.2 She's not prepared to help unless we'll pay her.
6.3 She won't be prepared to help unless we'd pay her.

7.1 If Jim talked less, he'd learn more.
7.2 If Jim would have talked less, he'd learn more.
7.3 If Jim has talked less, he'd learn more.

Our team would never have won ...

8.1 if they won't have so much support from the fans.
8.2 if they don't have so much support from the fans.
8.3 if they hadn't had so much support from the fans.
8.4 if they haven't had so much support from the fans.

Hast du das gekonnt?
Falls du nicht alle falschen Sätze identifiziert hast, mache weiter mit diesem Abschnitt (Seite 91).
Falls du die Aufgabe richtig lösen konntest, kannst du mit dem nächsten Abschnitt weitermachen (Seite 95).

➤ Es existieren verschiedene Arten von **if**-Sätzen und drei davon musst du dir vor allem merken. Stelle dir eine Waage vor:
In der linken Waagschale ist ein **if**-Satz und in der rechten ein Hauptsatz (der andere Satzteil). Du brauchst nur darauf zu achten, dass die Waagschalen immer im Lot sind – d.h. die Zeiten in den zwei Satzteilen müssen in der richtigen Kombination stehen. Da aber die Kombinationen der Zeiten bei den **if**-Sätzen feststehend sind, löst sich das Problem praktisch von selbst.

➤ **Typ I**
If the weather **gets** worse, I'**ll stay** at home.
(**if** + simple present; **will** / **can** / … + Infinitiv)

Übrigens: Anstelle von **if** … **not** benutzt man oft **unless**
If the weather does **not** get better, …
→ **Unless** the weather gets better, I'll stay at home.

➤ **Typ II**
If Marc **told** me the truth, I **would believe** him.
(**if** + simple past; **would** / **could** / … + Infinitiv)
Nicht: ~~If Marc would tell me the truth,~~ …
Wenn Marc mir die Wahrheit sagen würde, …

➤ **Typ III**
If I **had gone** to New York, I **would have visited** you.
(**if** + past perfect; **would** / **could** / … **have** + past participle)

Exercise 1 Vervollständige die folgenden Sätze mit einer passenden Form der Verben. Welche Art von if-Satz du benutzen musst ist jeweils angegeben.

1 If you ______________ me your video, I ____________________ it at the weekend. **Typ I:** *lend, use*

2 I think we ____________ the match if we ____________________ harder. **Typ I:** *lose, not train*

3 If Shakespeare ______________ alive today, he ____________ certainly ____________ a billionaire. **Typ II:** *be, be*

4 If she ________________ to speak with an American accent, she ______________________________ . **Typ II:** *try, not succeed*

5 Fewer tourists ____________ Britain if we ____________ ____________ a monarchy. **Typ II**: *visit, not have*

6 The UK's economy ____________ if we ____________ the EC in 1973.
Typ III: *could + suffer, not join*

7 Our situation ____________ better unless inflation ____________ to 3%. **Typ I**: *not get, fall*

8 The play ____________ far more successful if they ____________ some better actors.
Typ III: *might be, find*

9 If the United Nations ____________ , nobody ____________ solve the world's problems.
Typ II: *not exist, be able to*

10 ____________ the USA ____________ on the moon sooner if Congress ____________ more?
Typ III: *could + land, spend*

11 Mike ____________ the time to do it even if he ____________ work from 9-5.
Typ II: *never have, not have to*

12 I'm afraid I ____________ repair it unless somebody ____________ it first.
Typ I: *not be able to, explain*

13 If I ____________ you, I ____________ it with your wife. **Typ II**: *be, discuss*

14 Our plane ____________ earlier if it ____________ ____________ snowing. **Typ III**: *leave, not start*

15 If you ____________ me a chance, I ____________ ____________ you the whole story. **Typ II**: *give, can + tell*

··· Exam Tip 30 In einem **if-Satz** sind ***would*** und ***will*** praktisch **ausgeschlossen** außer in ein paar seltenen Fällen!
Sei daher besonders **vorsichtig** bei **Typ II** (siehe Exercise 2, Nr. 5–7), bei dem man im Deutschen häufig „würde(n)" benutzt.

··· Exam Tip 31 Im Englischen bevorzugt man ***were*** in einem **if-Satz**, bei dem man sonst **was** benutzen müsste, z.B.
*If I / he **were** the boss, ...* (vgl. die Lösung zu Exercise 1, Nr. 3).

··· Exam Tip 32 Steht der **if-Satz** am **Satzanfang**, muss er vom restlichen Satz durch ein **Komma** getrennt werden.

Exercise 2 Übersetze die farbigen Satzteile.

1 *Wenn ich Zeit habe, werde ich sie morgen anrufen.*

____

______________ her tomorrow.

2 *Sie wird nicht viel verdienen, wenn sie nicht härter arbeitet.*

____ much,

_____________________________________ harder.

3 *Wenn Custer die Schlacht am Little Big Horn gewonnen hätte, wäre er vielleicht Präsident der USA geworden.*

________________________________ the Battle of the Little

Bighorn, perhaps ____________________________ President.

4 *Wenn wir Skilaufen gehen, wenn das Wetter bis zum Wochenende besser wird.*

____

____

____

____

____

by the weekend.

5 *Wenn du das Buch lesen würdest, würdest du verstehen, was ich meine.* ______________________________

______________________________ what I mean.

6 *Wenn die Regierung uns geholfen hätte, hätten wir bessere Jobs bekommen.* ______________________________

______________________________ better jobs.

7 *Wenn Deutschland die EU verlassen würde, gäbe es viele Probleme für Europa.* ______________________________

______________ the EU, ______________________________

a lot of problems for Europe.

8 *Ich würde den „Klausurtrainer" kaufen, wenn ich du wäre!*

______________________ the "Klausurtrainer" ______________________

______________________ !

Exam Tip 33 Das Wort ***apartment*** schreibt sich im Englischen mit einem ***p***. Nicht mit der deutschen Schreibweise verwechseln!

B 17 Wortstellung: Was steht wo am besten?

Streiche jeden Satz, in dem die Wortstellung entweder falsch ist oder nicht die bestmögliche.

1.1 He's mean – he never offers to pay for anything.
1.2 He's mean – he offers never to pay for anything.
1.3 He's mean – he offers to never pay for anything.

2.1 Paul has refused often to take me skiing.
2.2 Paul has refused to take me skiing often.
2.3 Paul has often refused to take me skiing.

3.1 Marc sometimes had been late for school.
3.2 Marc had been sometimes late for school.
3.3 Marc had sometimes been late for school.

4.1 He spoke shyly about his new girlfriend.
4.2 He shyly spoke about his new girlfriend.

5.1 Jutta reads and writes well Italian.
5.2 Jutta well reads and writes Italian.
5.3 Well Jutta reads and writes Italian.
5.4 Jutta reads and writes Italian well.

6.1 The economy quickly will improve next year.
6.2 Next year the economy quickly will improve.
6.3 The economy will improve quickly next year.

7.1 Why does she every time behave that way?
7.2 Why does she behave every time that way?
7.3 Why does she behave that way every time?

8.1 The Americans already have sent men to the moon.
8.2 To the moon the Americans already have sent men.
8.3 Already to the moon the Americans have sent men.
8.4 The Americans have already sent men to the moon.

Hast du das gekonnt?
Falls du nicht jeweils die bestmögliche Lösung identifiziert hast, mache weiter mit diesem Abschnitt (Seite 96).
Falls du die Aufgabe richtig lösen konntest, mache weiter mit dem nächsten Abschnitt (Seite 98).

Exam Tip 34 Die bestmögliche Wortstellung im Englischen entspricht der Reihenfolge: **Art** und **Weise** / **Ort** / **Zeit**.
Das heißt auf Englisch: *manner* / *place* / *time*.
Merke dir den Spruch: "*More Pizza, Tina?*"

➤ Die englische Wortstellung ist flexibler als die deutsche und daher ist ein Wort oder eine Zusammensetzung an der falschen Stelle oft weniger störend (zumindest im Alltagsgebrauch) als im Deutschen.
Es geht im Folgenden um gängige **Adverbien** wie **easily**, sowie **Adverbialbestimmungen** wie **in a silly way** und **every month**.

➤ **unbestimmte Zeit / Häufigkeit**
already, **always**, **ever**, **frequently**, **just**, **mostly**, **normally**, **now**, **often**, **sometimes**, **soon**, **still**, **usually** stehen in der Regel:
vor dem 1. Hauptverb: I **never** eat meat.
nach dem 1. Hilfsverb: I have **never eaten** meat.
nach to be: I am **always** late.

➤ **bestimmte Zeit / Häufigkeit**
daily, **once**, **yearly**, **one year ago**, **October 25th**, **next week**, **every morning** stehen am Satzanfang oder häufiger am Satzende:
He drove to his office **every morning**. (Ort vor Zeit!)

yet, **before**, **a lot**, **very much** stehen auch am Satzende:
I've seen the film **before** – I didn't enjoy it **very much**.

Dies gilt in der Regel auch für Zusammensetzungen wie **as soon as possible**, **most of the time**, **now and again**.

➤ **Art und Weise**
angrily, **badly**, **carefully**, **quickly**, **slowly**, **shyly**, **well**
stehen in der Regel nach dem Verb (+ Objekt):
He drove **carefully**. / He drove the new car **carefully**.

Exercise Was steht wo am besten im Satz? Verbinde jeweils mit Pfeil(en) Adverb oder Adverbialbestimmung mit dem richtigen Kästchen.

1 Mahatma Gandhi ❑ was ❑ born ❑ ❑. ↝ *in India*, ↝ *in 1869*

2 Gandhi ❑ believed ❑ in non-violence. ↝ *always*

3 The name 'Mahatma' ❑ is ❑ translated ❑ as 'Great Soul'.

↝ *normally*

4 He ❑ was ❑ successful ❑ in avoiding violent confrontations. ⤳ *frequently*

5 ❑ The British ❑ reacted to Gandhi ❑. ⤳ *angrily*

6 No Indian thought it ❑ would ❑ be ❑ possible to have their own government. ⤳ *ever*

7 ❑ Gandhi was ❑ for ❑ for his non-violent protests. ⤳ *in prison*, ⤳ *several years*

8 He ❑ lived ❑ and ❑ he ❑ used ❑ to pray ❑. ⤳ *simply*, ⤳ *daily*

9 Many British people ❑ admired him ❑. ⤳ *very much*

10 ❑ Gandhi wanted ❑ the British ❑ to leave ❑ India ❑. ⤳ *as soon as possible*

11 ❑ India would not ❑ have become ❑ independent ❑ if Gandhi had not lived. ⤳ *maybe*, ⤳ *as early as 1947*

12 ❑ Gandhi was very anti-British, but he ❑ hated ❑ those who ruled his country ❑. ⤳ *obviously*, ⤳ *never*

13 Even ❑ Gandhi felt ❑ that independence ❑ was ❑ an impossible dream. ⤳ *now and again*

14 He ❑ was ❑ assassinated ❑ ❑ by Hindu fanatics *[Fanatiker]*. ⤳ *in New Delhi*, ⤳ *in 1948*

15 The 'Great Soul' ❑ is ❑ loved ❑ by Indians ❑. ⤳ *still*, ⤳ *everywhere*

··· Exam Tip 34 Folgende Adverbien stehen meistens am Satzanfang:
anyway*, *(un)fortunately*, *maybe*, *obviously*, *perhaps*, *probably*, *yet

··· Exam Tip 35 Merke dir die Schreibweise von folgenden Adverbien:
busily → *busy*, *easily* → *easy*, *basically* → *basic*,
economically → *economic*, *fantastically* → *fantastic*
Aber: *publicly* → *public*

B 18 Komma oder kein Komma?

Streiche jeden Satz, in dem ein Komma fehlt oder an der falschen Stelle steht.

1.1 Tea, coffee, and wine, are drinks, aren't they?
1.2 Tea, coffee, and wine are drinks, aren't they?
1.3 Tea coffee and wine are drinks, aren't they?
1.4 Tea coffee and wine are drinks aren't they?

2.1 India, Malaysia, etc. are Commonwealth countries.
2.2 India, Malaysia etc., are Commonwealth countries.
2.3 India, Malaysia etc. are Commonwealth countries.

3.1 Of course before I leave the UK, I'll call you.
3.2 Of course, before I leave the UK I'll call you.
3.3 Of course, before I leave the UK, I'll call you.

4.1 Until the economy improves, things will be hard.
4.2 Until the economy improves things will be hard.
4.3 Things will be hard, until the economy improves.
4.4 Things will be hard until the economy improves.

5.1 Unless prices drop by 3,5%, the PM will resign.
5.2 Unless prices drop by 3.5%, the PM will resign.
5.3 Unless prices drop by 3,5% the PM will resign.

6.1 Why not admit that you don't want to come?
6.2 Why not admit, that you don't want to come?
6.3 Why not admit, that, you don't want to come?

7.1 If we only knew, what to do, we'd do it.
7.2 If we only knew what to do we'd do it.
7.3 If we only knew, what to do we'd do it.
7.4 If we only knew what to do, we'd do it.

8.1 The only person who understands Swedish is Jim.
8.2 The only person who understands Swedish, is Jim.
8.3 The only person, who understands Swedish, is Jim.

Hast du das gekonnt?
Falls du nicht alle falschen Sätze identifiziert hast, mache weiter mit diesem Abschnitt (Seite 99).
Falls du die Aufgabe richtig lösen konntest, mache weiter mit dem Teil C (Seite 101).

Exam Tip 36 Nach der direkten Rede bleibt das **Komma** – im Gegensatz zum Deutschen – **innerhalb** der Anführungszeichen:
“Time for bed now,” said Chris to Jim.

➤ Zugegeben: Die Kommas sind in einer Klassenarbeit oder in einem Test nicht das Wichtigste. Die Grundlagen der Kommaregeln solltest du jedoch beherrschen, um zumindest Fehler in Relativsätzen und solch haarsträubende Schnitzer wie diesen zu vermeiden:
~~I'm quite sure, that Jakob is the guy, who did it.~~

➤ **Man setzt ein Komma** …

bei einer **Aufzählung** und vor einem **Frageanhägsel**:
Rain, fog, and snow are awful, **aren't they**?

bei **if** als erstem Satzteil sowie bei **(al)though**, **after**, **as**, **before**, **since**, **unless**, **until**, **when**, **while**:
If you help me, I'll help you.

vor **Abkürzungen** wie **e.g.**, **etc.**, **i.e.**, d.h.:
You'll need pen, paper, ink, **etc.** for the exam.

bei Wörtern wie **however**, **indeed**, **moreover** sowie **of course**, **in fact**, **for example**:
Nicola Anderson will be, **in fact**, our new president.

vor **und** nach einem **nicht bestimmenden Relativsatz**:
My mother, **who lives near Dover**, often visits Cornwall.

➤ **Man setzt kein Komma** …

vor **if**, wenn es den **zweiten Satzteil** einleitet. Diese Faustregel gilt auch für die Wörter **(al)though**, **after**, **as**, **before**, **since**, **unless**, **until**, **when**, **while**:
Nobody knows **if** Marylin Monroe killed herself or not.

vor **Infinitiven** und **that**-Satzteilen:
Perhaps you can tell me how **to explain** this.
She told me **that** it was very complicated.

vor einem **bestimmenden Relativsatz**:
She's one of the greatest writers **that I've ever read**.

in Dezimalzahlen:
3.54 (three **point** five four) im Gegensatz zum Deutschen: 3,54!

Exercise Richtig oder falsch? In jedem falschen Satz fehlt mindestens ein Komma – bessere diese Sätze entsprechend aus.

Arthur Conan Doyle, 1859–1930.

1 Sherlock Holmes who was created by the author Conan Doyle is probably the world's most famous detective.

2 Indeed the stories about Holmes are some of the most brilliant which have ever been written.

3 After Doyle had studied at Edinburgh University he started working as a doctor.

4 Holmes is based on a man called Dr Bell who taught medicine at Edinburgh.

5 While he was still a student Doyle had worked on a whaler *[Walfangschiff]* for a while.

6 Since however he had no patients 99.99% of the time he soon began to write detective stories.

7 Dr Doyle quickly became famous when he published six adventures about Holmes in 1891.

8 Sherlock Holmes is the first detective to use fingerprints for example in order to solve crimes.

9 Everybody has heard of *The Hound of the Baskervilles* which first appeared in a magazine from 1901-1902.

10 Anybody who has read it will have had lots of sleepless nights!

11 Sir Charles Baskerville who lives in his country house on Dartmoor is killed one night.

12 Even Holmes does not at first know what to do.

13 There are a number of things that make him think Sir Charles has been killed by a dog e.g. some huge footprints *[Fußabdruck]* near the body.

14 Of course you don't learn the truth until you reach the end of the book. (So if you want to read it I shan't tell you any more!)

C

C1 Tricky Exercise

Folgende 90 Sätze enthalten eine Mischung aus grundlegenden und doch z.T. kniffeligen Punkten im Englischen – typische Fehler, bei denen du schon einige Male ins Fettnäpfchen getreten bist. Wenn man den Klausurtrainer gründlich durchgearbeitet hat, sollte es nicht zu schwer sein, diesen Abschnitt erfolgreich zu bewältigen.

Markiere jeden Satz, in dem kein Fehler vorkommt.
Arbeite alle Seiten durch, bevor du die Lösungen anschaust.

1 It's about hundred miles to Penzance.
2 It's about a hundred miles to Penzance.
3 It's about thousand miles from here.
4 Nobody can lift thousand kilos.
5 Nobody can lift one thousand kilo.
6 Nobody can lift a thousand kilos.

7 All the quiz shows are stupid.
8 All quiz shows that I've ever watched are stupid.
9 All the quiz shows that I've ever watched are stupid.

10 Some foreigners don't know, that the Irish problem goes back centuries.
11 Others don't realize that the southern part of Ireland became independent in 1921.

12 If you read your history book, you'll understand better.
13 If there is peace soon everyone will be pleased.

14 The United States are a superpower.
15 The news is bad today.
16 The news yesterday were even worse.
17 The police has just arrived.
18 The police have just arrived.

19 Will you please stop talking all the time!
20 Will you please stop to talk all the time!
21 On the way he stopped to have lunch in Lower Tregantle.

22 I'll never forget how I saw Wall Street the first time.
23 I'll never forget seeing Wall Street the first time.
24 I'll never forget to see Wall Street the first time.

25 Will you remember to call me?
26 Will you remember calling me?
27 Jean remembered him calling her yesterday.
28 Don't forget to call Jean.

29 She suggested visiting the World Trade Center.
30 She suggested to visit the World Trade Center.

31 He would hate failing an English exam.
32 He'd hate to fail an English exam.

33 Some Scots would prefer to have their own separate government.
34 Years ago many of them liked having the Queen as head of state.
35 Angela said she had always loved to travel.

36 I would have come if she had been invited too.
37 I would have come if she would have been invited too.
38 I'll come if she'll be invited too.
39 I'll come if she's invited too.
40 I would come if she were invited too.
41 I would come if she would be invited too.

42 I'm looking for an accommodation in Bath, but I can not find a cheap appartment there.
43 I'm looking for an accomodation in Bath, but I can not find a cheap appartment there.
44 I'm looking for accommodation in Bath, but I cannot find a cheap apartment there.

45 The UN-delegation at the EU-conference wants to send NATO troops to Haiti.
46 The UN delegation at the EU conference wants to send NATO troops to Haiti.

47 Do you spell 'criticize' and 'address' like this?
48 Or do you spell 'critizize' and 'adress' like this?

49 They're of german nationality, I think.
50 That's a British car.

51 A two-year-old elephant can move a seven ton bus.
52 A two year-old elephant can move a seven-ton-bus.
53 A two-year-old elephant can move a seven-ton bus.

54 He's seventy six and still has no self confidence.
55 He's seventy-six and still has no selfconfidence.
56 He's seventy-six and still has no self-confidence.

57 It's a well known route.
58 The route is well known.

59 His carreer developped fast untill he was assasinated by a collegue.
60 His carrer developped fast until he was assassinated by a colleage.

61 His career developed fast until he was assassinated by a colleague.
62 His career develloped fast until he was asassinated by a coleague.

63 What a nonsense he talks the most time.
64 What nonsense talks he the most time.
65 What nonsense talks he the most of the time.
66 What a nonsense he talks most of the time.
67 What nonsense he talks most of the time.

68 The most people would keep such a thing as souvenir.
69 Most of the people would keep such a thing as souvenir.
70 Most people would keep such a thing as a souvenir.

71 She told that she had done it.
72 She said that she had done it.
73 She said me that she had done it.
74 She explained me that she had done it.
75 She said to me that she had done it.

76 What means this word in Russian?
77 Brian don't speak Hindi.

78 Basically your idea is easyly the best I've heard.
79 Basicly your idea is easyly the best I've heard.
80 Basically your idea is easily the best I've heard.

Ersetze jeweils das falsch verwendete Wort in den folgenden Sätzen:

81 Our Jumbo will start at precisely 7 o'clock.
82 Violence is a serious actual problem.
83 She became a child at the age of eighteen.
84 Jutta will become a job in the Philippines.
85 Eireen made a Latin exam yesterday.
86 Jakob made a photo of Sarah and won a prize.
87 Computers are the heart of modern technique.
88 He took part in the advertising action.
89 It's the worst note I've ever had at school.
90 Policy is a dirty business in my opinion.

Arbeite alle Sätze sorgfältig durch.
Solltest du nicht wissen, warum ein bestimmter Satz richtig bzw. falsch ist, so lese die entsprechende Erklärung auf Seite 105.
Du wirst dabei viele **Exam Tips** wiedererkennen.
Die Nummern beziehen sich auf die jeweiligen Beispielsätze.

1–6 Vorsicht bei dem *s* in *two pounds*, *six dollars*, etc.
Vorsicht auch bei Zahlen wie:
hundert – *a /one hundred*; tausend – *a /one thousand*

7–9 *all the ...* bedeutet alle aus einer bestimmten Anzahl, z.B.
***All the** teachers **in this school** are friendly.*
Meint man ***all*** ganz allgemein, benutzt man kein ***the***.

10–11 **Niemals ein Komma** im Englischen vor *that* im Sinne von dass.

12–13 Steht der if-Satz am Satzanfang, **muss** er vom restlichen Satz durch ein **Komma getrennt** werden.

14–18 Wörter wie ***the United States***, ***news***, etc. werden immer als Singular behandelt. ***Police*** wird immer als Plural behandelt:
Die Polizei ist da. – *The police **are** here.*

19–21 Bedeutungsunterschied bei Infinitiv und Gerundium:
stop *+ -ing* – aufhören, etwas zu tun;
stop *+ Infinitiv* – anhalten, um etwas (anderes) zu tun.

22–30 Nach den Verben ***remember*** und ***forget*** steht immer ein Infinitiv (oder bei Vorzeitigkeit ein Gerundium) und **nicht**
~~*remember / forget + how ...*~~
Ich erinnere mich, wie ich L.A. zum ersten Mal sah.
*I **remember seeing** L.A. for the first time.*
Übrigens: ***suggest*** steht immer mit ***-ing!***

31–35 Nach ***like***, ***love***, ***hate***, ***prefer*** unterscheidet man heute kaum noch zwischen Infinitiv und Gerundium.
Would like / ***love*** / ***hate*** / ***prefer*** jedoch immer mit **Infinitiv**!

36–41 In einem if-Satz sind ***would*** und ***will*** praktisch ausgeschlossen, außer in ein paar seltenen Fällen! Sei deshalb besonders vorsichtig bei **Typ II**, bei dem man im Deutschen häufig „würde(n)“ benutzt.
Im Englischen bevorzugt man ***were*** in einem if-Satz, wo man sonst **was** benutzen müßte, z.B. *If I / he **were** the boss, ...*

42–62 Wenn man im Deutschen **eine Unterkunft** sagt, spricht man im Englischen fast immer von *accommodation* ohne den Artikel *a*.

Es gibt im Englischen fast **nie einen Bindestrich** bei Abkürzung plus Substantiv:
UN-Truppen – ***UN troops***, NATO-Konferenz – ***NATO conference***, etc.

Bei Wörtern wie ***self**-confidence* – Selbstbewußtsein ist ein **Bindestrich immer notwendig**.

Er steht auch bei **Zahlen** wie ***thirty-two, sixty-five*** und folgenden typischen Zusammensetzungen:
*a **two-year-old** child, a **fifty-pound** note, a **well-known** author*
(immer mit Bindestrich vor einem Substantiv).
Aber: *He is **well known**.*
Weitere Stolpersteine: *apartment, a**dd**re**ss**, criti**c**ize,*
*develo**p**ed → develo**p**, car**ee**r, a**ss**a**ss**inate, coll**eague**.*
(Und ***cannot*** – ein Wort.)

Nationalitätsbezeichnungen werden immer groß geschrieben wie ***French***, ...

63–70 arbeiten als Lehrer, ... – *to work as **a** teacher, ...*
Was für **ein** Unsinn! – *What nonsense!*
Die meisten Leute – *most people;*
die meiste Zeit – *most of **the** time*

71–75 Nach ***tell*** kein ***that***-Satz von der Art:
~~*He told that he had seen it*~~.
Merke Dir auch ***explain** / **say** sth. **to** someone*

76–77 Bilde niemals solche Sätze auf Englisch wie,
~~*Like you muesli?, Speaks he Hindi?*~~
Hier ist eine Form von ***do*** erforderlich:
***Do** you **like** muesli?, **Does** he **speak** Hindi?*

78–80 Merke dir die Schreibweise von folgenden Adverbien:
*eas**ily** ↔ eas**y**, bus**ily** ↔ bus**y**,*
*basic**ally** ↔ basic, economic**ally** ↔ economic,*
*fantastic**ally** ↔ fantastic.*
Aber: *public**ly** ↔ public.*

81–90 Hier handelt es sich um typische Wortverwechslungen, die man alle einzeln lernen muss.

C2 Mixed Exercise

Verbessere die Fehler – die zwischen den Brillen kursiv gedruckt sind – in dieser Klassenarbeit.

Thanksgiving Day in America.

In the winter of 1620 the first group of English families, the Pilgrims, *are arrived* ________________ in Plymouth, Massachusetts, after a long and difficult journey in their ship, the Mayflower.

That first winter was even *more bad* ________________ than the journey by ship for them, because it was very *coldly* ________________ and they had very *few* ________________ food. *much* ________________ of them died, and *all were* ________________ very glad when spring finally came.

Indians *lived* ________________ there when the Pilgrims *were arriving,* ________________ and *lucky,* ________________ they were very friendly and *helpfully* ________________ . They *have been teaching* ________________ the Europeans about the new things *what* ________________ they had never seen before – corn, turkey, cranberries, sweet potatoes. After the first harvest, life was *very* ________________ *more good* ________________ for the Pilgrims, they were *more healthy and happy* ________________ as ________________ they had been a year before, so they *were having* ________________ a big feast and invited their friends the Indians, and *have thanked* ________________ them and God.

Thanksgiving Day became so important in New England because in the early days of the colonies the Puritans *which* ________________ lived there *used to thinking* ________________

Christmas was too worldly and bad to celebrate. So people got *used to have* ________________ big Thanksgiving feasts in November instead.

Since 1863 Thanksgiving *is* ________________ a National holiday. In the middle of the Civil War, Abraham Lincoln *has thought* ________________ it would help *all* ________________ to live together *peacefuller* ________________ . At any rate, *since* ________________ over 230 years now, Americans *are cooking* ________________ big turkey dinners and are having family celebrations on this day.

Now Thanksgiving is also famous for a time for American football. Usually the men *are watching* ________________ the game on TV and the women *watch not* ________________ the game, but *are taking* ________________ care of the food in the kitchen.

a lot ________________ people *are believing* ________________ ________________ these days that this is not the way it *had better* ________________ ________________ be – men and women *shall* ________________ do both things together. A *little* ________________ modern families these days *let the dinner make* ________________ ________________ for them by a restaurant or a party service.

C 3 Übersetzungstest

Übersetze die Sätze. Falls du Schwierigkeiten hast, kannst du jeweils im angegebenen Kapitel nachschlagen.

1 *Normalerweise arbeite ich in einem Kaufhaus, aber diesen Monat arbeite ich auf dem Flohmarkt.* ↝ B1

____

____

2 *Er wohnt in Obermenzing. Er ist seit November unsere Englischlehrer. Wir lesen seit vier Wochen „Moby Dick" mit ihm.* ↝ B2

____

____

3 *Romeo war dabei einen Kuchen zu backen, als Juliet nach Hause kam.* ↝ B3 ____________________

____

____

____

4 *Die Stadt hat in letzter Zeit viele neue Wohnungen gebaut. John hat letzte Woche ein schönes Haus in Cranton gesehen.* ↝ B4

____

____

____

____

5 *Sie putzt seit einer Stunde Gemüse und gerade hat sie sich geschnitten.* ↝ B5 ______________________________

____

6 *Ich würde gern aufhören zum Jazztanz zu gehen, aber ich genieße es immer, nachher mit der Gruppe Tee zu trinken.* B9

____

____

7 *Das Team hat in letzter Zeit ziemlich schwer gearbeitet, aber sie haben trotzdem schlecht gespielt.* B10 _______________

____

____

8 *Dieser Fernseher ist größer und viel teurer als die andere zwei, aber er hat schlechtere Farben als sie und ist am kompliziertesten zu bedienen.* B11 _______________

____

____

9 *Es ist nicht viel Geld in der Kasse, aber wir haben viel Zeit vor dem Fest und wir können selber ziemlich viel Kuchen backen und ein wenig Punsch machen.* B13 _______________

____

____

10 *Es kommt jemand, um die Heizung zu reparieren, aber es gibt niemanden, der die Türen streichen kann. Fast alle sind in Urlaub.* B14 _______________

____

11 *Normalerweise feiert er seinen Geburtstag am 5. Mai, aber dieses Jahr hat er schon früher, am 3. Mai, gefeiert.* B17

____

____

12 *Wenn er mir etwas gesagt hätte, hätte ich ihm geholfen. Falls er sich beschwert, sag ich ihm das.* ↝ B16 ______________________

____

____

13 *Früher pflegte ich mein eigenes Auto zu reparieren, aber ich bin nicht mehr gewöhnt, es selbst zu tun.* ↝ B8

____

____

____

____

14 *Diese Medizin soll sehr gut sein, aber ich persönlich glaube das nicht. Du solltest zu einem anderen Arzt gehen. Soll ich einen für dich suchen?* ↝ B7 ______________________

____

____

15 *Ich werde es nicht zulassen, dass du diese schweren Taschen schleppst. Wir lassen sie abholen.* ↝ B6

____

____

16 *Mein Vater, der immer bereit ist für andere zu kochen, plant gerade ein Essen, das zwölf Gänge haben wird.* ↝ B15

____

____

17 *Die meisten Leute finden Urlaub in Sommer wunderbar, aber ich würde gern zur Abwechslung Urlaub im Januar machen.* ↝ B12

____

____

C4 Finde den Fehler

Die Zahl hinter der Brille zeigt dir, wie viele Fehler es in jedem Satz gibt. Kreise jeden Fehler ein, dann schreibe die Korrekturen unter den Satz.

1 He has given me a usefully advice two month ago. 4

____

2 Stays Bill usually at pensions when he travel? 3

____

3 How much students know people which are good photographs? 3 ______________________________

4 Their's not something I can do for him if he will refuse giving up to smoke. 5 ______________________________

____

5 You are becoming our goods quick when we receive your payment on time. 4 ______________________________

____

6 She is drinking never tea to the breakfast, or? 4

____

7 Who likes not these strawberry marmelade? 3

____

8 I live in Germany now since seven years, but I lived in Tokyo when they were having that earthquake *[Erdbeben]*. 4

____

____

9 Have you ever been drinking irish beer? Yes, I have done it last June when we have been in Ireland. 4 ______________________________

____

10 We're fed up to compare prices. We know that their CD's are always expensiver as our. 4

11 When you will be interested for our product, we sent you a catalogue. 4

12 She is used to sing so beautiful like Maria Callas, but these days she has very few time to practise. 4

13 She's the tourist, which has the least bags. 3

14 I just been to a beach who there are as much surfers like on this one. 4

15 He often play tennis more bad as his students. 3

16 There stand any bottles of milk in the fridge. We'll tell all, so they don't bring more. 4

17 I let always my car repair there. Their mechanics can it very good. 5

18 Don't worry! I am used to explain her, that a lot of changes are neccesary. 4

19 If I would have worked as secretary, I had earned three thousands in two month. 4

C 5 Mixed Exercise

Finde und verbessere die Fehler in diesem Bewerbungsschreiben.

My name is Britta Deutschmann and I am coming from Germany. I have stopped to go to gymnasium for two years, but I didn't become my Abitur yet. After finished school I have worked in a restaurant as cook for one year. I stopped to do this work while the restaurant closed. Since ten months I am working by a large company on the production line, but I like not my job very much. We must to work hardly, and it is a bored job.
So I will have a new job as au pair with a sympathetic family. I enjoy to cook and do housework, and I am especially good to look for children. I take care of often my neighbour's children. I am a hobby photograph and I'm interesting for wildlife and much kinds of sports. I can spanish very good and a little english, and look forward to improve my english knowledges. It is most important second language in today's world. I think the job of au pair is one what could help me learn more good english. I hope very, that you can help me.

Lösungen

A

A1 Singular oder Plural

Richtig: 1.2, 2.3, 3.1, 4.2, 5.2, 6.1, 7.3, 8.2, 9.2

Exercise 1

1 damage / has
2 My binoculars / are lying
3 His knowledge of French / was
4 A good piece of advice / helps
5 Your good advice / was
6 is / the news
7 the proof / wasn't
8 explain it to her
9 did she translate
10 The United States / possesses
11 Most people enjoy
12 The goods / weigh
13 Does he understand / doesn't he speak
14 Politics / is
15 work as a nurse
16 some new information / has

Exercise 2

1 Good furniture is often quite expensive.
2 The surroundings aren't very nice here.
3 Please explain the story to me again.
4 No news is good news.
5 Two pounds of apples cost four marks.
6 His hair was long and blond.

A2 Wörter, die man leicht wechselt

Richtig: 1.1, 2.1, 3.2, 4.2, 5.3, 6.2, 7.3, 8.3, 10.1, 11.3

Exercise 1

1 He reminds me of
2 Do you remember
3 He laid
4 borrow the money from the bank
5 Can you lend me your Oasis CD?
6 raise
7 The standard of living rose
8 I will receive
9 We appreciate
10 I estimate the price
11 Can you take
12 Check
13 It has been lying

Exercise 2

1 make
2 make
3 take / do
4 have
5 take

Exercise 3

1 technology
2 technique
3 serious
4 permission
5 permit
6 crisps / chips
7 road / street
8 great / fat
9 economic
10 economical
11 husband
12 employee, employer
13 wife

Exercise 4

1 as soon as possible / as carefully as possible
2 He is exactly like me
3 Workers like us
4 No, none of the four.
5 No, neither of them.
6 Firstly / first
7 At first / few friends / a few of the girls
8 lose / lost

A3 Falsche Freunde

Richtig: 1.2 ,1.4, 2.3, 3.4, 4.2, 5.2, 5.4, 6.3, 6.4, 7.1, 7.3, 8.1, 8.3

Exercise 1

1 your opinion
2 This meaning
3 Our grammar school / a very modern gymnasium
4 a very sensible idea
5 Actually / current
6 The actual danger
7 get / university
8 a high school
9 a well-behaved, very sensitive boy
10 to work in a labaratory
11 a small guest-house / pension
12 brave / likeable
13 consistent
14 marmelade / jam
15 old alleys / elegant avenues

Exercise 2

1 falsch – Every Christian believes in Christ.
2 falsch – The current advertising campaign will be expensive.
3 falsch – Who's the boss of your company?
4 falsch – She acted consistently, and that's why she's been successful.
5 richtig
6 falsch – We design PCs in our laboratory.
7 richtig
8 richtig
9 falsch – She's always dressed in the current fashion.
10 falsch – The murderer went to prison for murder.

A4 Gleiche Aussprache – Unterschiedliche Schreibweise

Richtig: 1.3, 2.3, 3.2, 4.3, 5.2, 6.1, 7.4, 8.2, 9.2, 10.2

Exercise

1 falsch – He began the letter with "Dear Sir or Madam".
2 falsch – It's not fair to expect people to pay such a high price for a ticket to the fair next week.
3 falsch – Great Britain's whole economy depends very much on its oil production.
4 falsch – I heard or read somewhere that red is a colour which, in China, is supposed to bring good luck.
5 falsch – There's only one piece of cake left, I'm afraid.
6 falsch – There are herds of deer all over Scotland. We saw lots of them when we drove through the Highlands.

A5 Rechtschreibung mit Tücken

Richtig: 1.3, 2.4, 3.3, 4.3, 5.3, 6.4, 7.2

Exercise 1
1 rebels
2 emigrants / immigrants
3 career / success
4 assassinated / commit
5 parallel / straight
6 whether / belief / proof
7 fourteen / forty

Exercise 2
1 falsch – Marc has no self-confidence in spite of the fact that he's a well-known singer.
2 falsch – He's Irish, sixty-five years old and an ex-policeman.
3 falsch – People were surprised, even annoyed, to hear that sort of advice from the director, but no-one realised thar he was actually joking.
4 falsch – I cannot seriously believe that another ten-mile walk at the weekend will help me to lose weight, although I certainly need more exercise.
5 falsch – Dear Dr West, You have been chosen to attend the UN conference in Berlin as part of the UK delegation.

Exercise 3
1 According to the calendar / Sunday / on Sundays
2 Two of my colleagues / in the choir
3 medicine / poisonous
4 Is it a Jewish or a Muslim
5 The thief / two cheques
6 separate tables

Exercise 4
1 canoe
2 ceiling
3 to receive
4 pronounciation
5 to queue
6 cocoa
7 niece
8 to lose

Exercise 5
1 The word is nearly unpronouncable.
2 The new assistant is reliable, confident and efficient.
3 Claudia is beautiful and successful.
4 Wait until (till) I come.
5 The plan is admirable but unimaginable.
Are you responsible for it?

A6 Einfacher oder doppelter Konsonant
Richtig: 1.2, 2.4, 3.3, 4.1, 5.3, 6.1

Exercise
1 falsch – They were robbed while they were travel(l)ing through Florida.
2 falsch – The firm is offering me another chance to be their official representative in London. I've been chosen from more than 100 candidates.
3 falsch – I cannot imagine that the new dress fitted her.
4 falsch – These biscuits are absolutely delicious.
5 falsch – We paid quite a lot to get into the Science Museum after we had been queueing for half an hour.
6 falsch – There's been a terrible disaster in an area south of here which is controlled by US troops.
7 richtig
8 falsch – She comes from a family of immigrants who emigrated from Ireland in 1925.
9 richtig
10 falsch – There is no proof that King Arthur ever lived.

A7 Hilfsverben
Richtig: 1.1, 1.3, 2.1, 3.2, 4.2, 5.2, 5.4, 6.3, 6.5, 7.3, 8.3

Exercise
1 He doesn't like Hamburgers and Jane doesn't either.
2 What do you have for breakfast every day?
Who makes your breakfast?
3 How many people would like to go to the concert?
How much are the tickets?
4 Can you speak French?
5 Yes, I can speak French, so does Traudl but Bruce doesn't and neither does Mark
6 She is very friendly isn't she?
7 We haven't paid enough yet or have we?
8 We shouldn't go by car (take the car), should we?
9 He goes to work every day, doesn't he?
10 You've made a few mistakes, haven't you?

B

B1 Simple present oder present progressive?
Richtig: 1.1, 2.1, 3.2, 4.1, 5.1, 6.2, 7.1, 8.1, 9.1, 10.1, 11.1

Exercise 1
helps, teaches, travels, is training, is attending, is giving, arrives, travels, is having, loses

Exercise 2
thinks, tells, is trying, is having, is thinking, loves, doesn't want, has, believes

B2 Present oder present perfect progressive?
Richtig: 1.2, 1.4, 2.1, 3.1, 4.1, 5.1

Exercise
1 Tom and Jerry are playing poker.
2 How long have they been playing poker?
3 I'm exhausted. I've been painting the kitchen since 7 o' clock this morning.
4 I live in Cairo. (I'm living in Cairo.)
5 Do you really? How long have you been living there?
6 Is that so? I've been thinking for years that she is his secretary.
7 Is it not finished yet? He's been working on this old house for years.
8 Of course I know him. I've known him for years.
9 How long have you been here in Florence?
10 I haven't been playing the piano for long.
Only since March.

B3 Simple past or past progressive?
Richtig: 1.1, 2.2, 3.1, 4.1, 5.1, 6.1

Exercise
was baking, put, went, came, stole, was shopping, were staying, were watching, asked, were doing, were playing, finished, came, knocked, gave, looked

B4 Present perfect oder simple past?
Richtig: 1.1, 2.1, 3.1, 4.1, 5.1, 6.1, 7.1, 8.1, 9.1, 10.1, 11.1

Exercise
told, haven't found, finished, started, has been forced, haven't been, have decided, have always enjoyed, have never lived, have had, worked, lived, took, enjoyed, invited, have written, have had

B5 Present perfect simple oder progressive?
Richtig: 1.1, 2.1, 2.2, 3.2, 4.1, 5.1, 6.2, 7.1, 8.1, 9.1, 10.1, 11.1, 11.2

Exercise
1 burnt
2 worked / been working
3 been playing
4 been looking
5 packed
6 known
7 done
8 been painting
9 been learning
10 written / sent

B6 Let, make, get / have something done
Richtig: 1.3, 2.1, 2.4, 3.1, 4.1, 5.1, 5.2, 6.1

Exercise
They don't force us to, we were forced to, allow us to go (let us go), allow us to (let us), get (have) the staff to bring us a snack and coffee, had my back and feet massaged, they made us pay, to have it done, let the new employees practise, I'm going to have my horoscope done next week, get her to do yours, I'll get her to call you next week

B7 Shall, should, be supposed to, ought to, had better
Richtig: 1.2, 2.1, 3.1, 3.2, 4.2, 5.1, 6.1, 7.1

Exercise
shouldn't (had better not), ought to, shall, are supposed to, ought, had better, is said, shall, ought to (should)

B8 Used to do, used to doing, get used to
Richtig: 1.1, 2.1, 2.3, 3.2, 4.2, 5.1, 5.2, 6.2, 7.3, 8.1, 9.1, 9.4

Exercise
had, lived, worked, are not used to working, worked, went, travelled, always had to do, used to work, were, aren't used to living, left, had, sold, moved, used to be, married, was, could get used to milking, feeding

B9 Gerundium oder Infinitiv?
Richtig: 1.2, 2.3, 3.3, 4.1, 5.3, 6.1, 6.2, 7.1, 7.2, 8.2

Exercise 1
1 richtig (kann aber auch mit Gerund stehen)
2 falsch – His films are certainly worth watching – some people consider him to be a genius and everybody expects him to win an Oscar.
3 falsch – There's no sense in carrying on studying French much longer if you dislike learning foreign languages.
4 hier geht auch – I hate to talk in front of lots of people – I'd prefer to avoid situations like that.
5 falsch – Paul is considering looking for a new position. If the company refuses to give him money, he'll probably stop working for them.
6 falsch – Would you mind closing the window, please?
7 falsch – If we manage to make a profit again, people will continue to invest.

Exercise 2
1 against travelling
2 of / winning
3 on getting
4 of being
5 up with trying / at explaining
6 in reaching / to working
7 of becoming / of doing

Exercise 3
1 Please don't forget to call him
2 Stop talking so much nonsense!
3 I will never forget flying
4 Uli couldn't stop laughing
5 Remember to inform him immediately.
6 Everybody remembers / losing

B10 Adjektiv oder Adverb?
Richtig: 1.1, 1.3, 2.1, 3.1, 4.2, 4.4, 5.1, 6.2, 7.2, 8.1, 8.2, 9.1, 9.3, 10.1

Exercise
1 early / quickly / slowly
2 painful / difficult
3 quite / hard / very well
4 beautifully / yearly / fantastic
5 Suddenly / terrible
6 unfortunately / expensive / secretly
7 nice / generous / pretty
8 quickly / quietly / carefully

B11 Die Steigerung von Adjektiven und Adverben
Richtig: 1.1, 2.1 3.2, 4.2, 5.1, 6.2, 7.2, 8.1, 9.4

Exercise
1 furthest
2 better than
3 the best / the worst
4 as large as
5 more expensive than / easier
6 more comfortable than
7 the biggest / the quietest
8 the loveliest / more interesting than

B12 Mit oder ohne Artikel?
Richtig: 1.3, 2.2, 3.1, 4.3, 5.2, 6.3, 7.2, 8.2

Exercise 1
1 the East End
2 Aunt Mary / at university
3 in the school / in June
4 St Paul's cathedral / the Strand
5 the USA / 10 Downing Street
6 As a girl / Switzerland / World War II / a Jew / as a subway driver
7 richtig
8 richtig
9 bread / the bread
10 Mount Everest
11 a hundred dollars
12 a Dutchman / the Netherlands
13 Queen Victoria

Exercise 2
1 in a loud voice
2 a thousand dollars a month
3 As a rule I smoke a pipe.
4 in case / at work
5 Most of the time / lying in bed, talking on the telephone
6 I'm in a hurry / half a day

7 What a pity / on (the) television
8 on the radio
9 Most people had a headache
10 he played the guitar and the piano
11 On Wednesday / without interruption
12 What nonsense

B13 Zählbare oder nicht zählbare Substantive

Richtig: 1.2, 1.3, 2.1, 2.2, 3.3, 4.1, 5.1, 5.2, 6.1, 7.1, 7.3, 8.1, 9.1

Exercise 1

so much, a few, a lot of, some, a few, a little, a lot of, too little, quite a lot of, lots of, many, very few, very little, many, much, have none

Exercise 2

the most, a few more, many more, fewer, less, the least, the fewest

B14 Zusammensetzungen mit some, any, every

Richtig: 1.1, 2.1, 3.1, 3.2, 4.1, 5.1, 6.1, 7.1, 7.3, 8.1, 9.1

Exercise 1

something, anything, anyone, any, some, anywhere, something, anything, any, any

Exercise 2

everybody, nobody, everybody says, everywhere, is everyone, all of you, everything

B15 Bestimmende oder nicht bestimmende Relativsätze

Richtig: 1.1, 2.1, 2.2, 3.1, 3.2, 4.2, 4.3, 5.1, 5.2, 6.1, 7.3, 8.1

Exercise 1

1 who taught music at our school last year
2 , which made things a bit difficult
3 , which was composed by Antonio Vivaldi
4 which is very similar to Vivaldi's Four Seasons
5 , which is called the Japanese Four Seasons
6 who my father is talking to
7 who spent a year at Mr Nagasaki's school in Japan
8 , where he lived
9 , who organizes the teacher exchange programmes
10 which I took at the concert
11 when my camera wasn't working very well

Exercise 2

1, 4, 6, 7, 10

B16 If-Sätze

Richtig: 1.4, 2.3, 3.2, 4.2, 5.1, 6.1, 7.1, 8.3

Exercise 1

1 lend / will use
2 will lose / don't train
3 were / would be
4 tried / would not succeed
5 would visit / didn't have
6 could have suffered had not joined
7 will not get / falls
8 might have been / had found
9 did not exist / would be able to
10 Could / have landed / had spent
11 would never have / didn't have to
12 will not be able to / explains
13 were / would
14 would have left / had not started
15 gave / could have told

Exercise 2

1 If I have the time, I will call
2 She won't earn / if she doesn't work
3 If Custer had won, he would have become
4 We can go skiing, if the weather gets better
5 If you had the book, you would understand
6 If the government had helped us, we would have got
7 If Germany left, there would be
8 I would buy / if I were you

B17 Wortstellung: Was steht wo am besten?

Richtig: 1.1, 2.3, 3.3, 4.1, 5.4, 6.3, 7.3, 8.4

Exercise

1 Mahatma Gandhi was born in India in 1869.
2 Gandhi always believed in non-violence.
3 The name Mahatma is normally translated as 'Great Soul'.
4 He was frequently successful in avoiding violent confrontations.
5 The British reacted to Gandhi angrily.
6 No Indian thought it would ever be possible to have their own government.
7 Gandhi was in prison for several years for his non-violent protests.
8 He lived simply and he used to pray daily.
9 Many British people admired him very much.
10 Gandhi wanted the British to leave India as soon as possible.
11 Maybe India would not have become independent as early as 1947 if Gandhi had not lived.
12 Obviously Gandhi was very anti-British, but he never hated those who ruled his country.
13 Even Gandhi felt now and again that independence was an impossible dream.
14 He was assassinated in New Delhi in 1948 by Hindu fanatics.
15 The 'Great Soul' is still loved by Indians everywhere.

B18 Komma oder kein Komma?

Richtig: 1.2, 2.1, 3.2, 4.1, 4.4, 5.2, 6.1, 7.4, 8.1

Exercise

1 Sherlock Holmes, who was created by the author Conan Doyle, is probably the world's most famous detective.
2 Indeed, the stories about Holmes are some of the most brilliant which have ever been written.
3 After Doyle had studied at Edinburgh University, he started working as a doctor.
4 Holmes is based on a man called Dr Bell, who taught medicine at Edinburgh.
5 While he was still a student, Doyle had worked on a whaler for a while.
6 Since, however, he had no patients 99.99% of the time, he soon began to write detective stories.
7 Dr Doyle quickly became famous when he published six adventures about Holmes in 1891.
8 Sherlock Holmes is the first detective to use fingerprints, for example, in order to solve crimes.
9 Everybody has heard of The Hound of the Baskervilles, which first appeared in a magazine from 1901-1902.
10 Anybody who has read it will have had lots of sleepless nights.
11 Sir Charles Baskerville, who lives in his country house on Dartmoor, is killed one night.
12 Even Holmes does not at first know what to do.
13 There are a number of things that make him think Sir Charles has been killed by a dog, e.g. some huge footprints near the body.
14 Of course, you don't learn the truth until you reach the end of the book. (So if you want to read it, I shan't tell you any more!)

C

C1 Tricky Exercise
Richtig: 2, 6, 9, 11, 12, 15, 18, 19, 21, 23, 25, 27, 28, 29, 32, 33, 34, 35, 36, 39, 40, 44, 46, 47, 50, 53, 56, 58, 61, 67, 70, 72, 75, 80,
81 take off,
82 current,
83 had,
84 get,
85 took / sat / did,
86 took,
87 technology,
88 campaign,
89 mark / grade,
90 Politics

C2 Mixed Exercise
arrived, worse, cold, little, Many / A lot, everybody was / all of them were, were living, arrived, luckily, helpful, taught, which / that / –, much, better, healthier and happier, than, had, thanked, who, used to think, used to having, has been, thought, everybody, more peacefully, for, have been cooking, watch, don't watch, take, A lot of, believe, should, should, few, have dinner made

C3 Übersetzungstest
1 Usually I work in a department store, but this month I'm working at a flea market.
2 He lives in Obermenzing. He has been our English teacher since November. We've been reading Moby Dick with him for four weeks.
3 Romeo was in the kitchen baking a cake when Juliet came home.
4 The city has built a lot of new flats recently. John saw a nice house in Cranton last week.
5 She has been cleaning vegetables for an hour and has just cut herself.
6 I'd like to give up going to Jazz-dance, but I always enjoy drinking tea with the group afterwards.
7 The team has been working quite hard recently, but they played badly anyway.
8 This television is bigger and more expensive than the other two, but it has worse colours than them and is the most complicated to operate.
9 There isn't much money in the cashbox, but we have a lot of time before the party and we can bake quite a lot of cakes and make a little punch ourselves.
10 Somebody is coming to repair the heating, but there's nobody / no one who can paint the doors. Almost everybody is on holiday.
11 Usually he celebrates his birthday on 5 May, but this year he celebrated earlier, on 3 May.
12 If he had said something to me, I would have helped him. In case he complains, tell him that.
13 I used to repair my own car, but I'm not used to doing it anymore.
14 This medicine is supposed to be / is said to be very good, but personally I don't believe it. You should / had better get / go to another doctor. Shall I find one for you?
15 I won't let you carry these heavy bags. We'll have them picked up.
16 My father, who is always ready to cook for others, is planning a meal which will have twelve courses.
17 Most people think holidays in summer are wonderful, but I would like to have a holiday in January for a change.

C4 Finde den Fehler
Die farbig hervorgehobenen Teile zeigen, was im Original falsch war. Manchmal muss man allerdings genauer hinsehen, da in den Sätzen Artikel oder Kommas zu viel waren.

1 He gave me useful advice two months ago.
2 Does Bill usually stay at bed and breakfasts when he travels?
3 How many students know people who are good photographers?
4 There's not anything / nothing I can do for him if he refuses to give up smoking.
5 You will get our goods quickly if we receive your payment on time.
6 She never drinks tea for breakfast, does she?
7 Who doesn't like this strawberry jam?
8 I have been living in Germany now for seven years, but I was living in Tokyo when they had that earthquake *[Erdbeben]*.
9 Have you ever drunk Irish beer? Yes, I did it last June when we were in Ireland.
10 We're fed up comparing prices. We know that their CD's are always more expensive than ours.
11 If you are interested in our product, we will send you a catalogue.
12 She used to sing as beautifully as her, but these days she has very little time to practise.
13 She's the tourist who has the fewest bags.
14 I have just been to a beach where there are as many surfers as on this one.
15 He often plays tennis worse than his students.
16 There are some bottles of milk in the fridge. We should tell everybody so they don't bring more.
17 I always have my car repaired there. Their mechanics can do it very well.
18 Don't worry! I am used to explaining to her that a lot of changes are necessary.
19 If I had worked as a secretary, I would have earned three thousand in two months.

C5 Ein Brief
My name is Britta Deutschmann and I come from Germany. I stopped going to grammar school two years ago, but I haven't received / got my Abitur (diploma) yet. After finishing school I worked in a restaurant as a cook for one year. I stopped doing this work because the restaurant closed. For ten months I have been working for a large company on the production line, but I don't like my job very much. We have to work hard, and it is a boring job. So I would like to have a new job as an au pair with a nice family. I enjoy cooking and doing housework, and I am especially good at looking after children. I often take care of my neighbour's children. I am a hobby photographer and I'm interested in wildlife and many kinds of sports. I can speak Spanish very well and a little English, and look forward to improving my knowledge of English. It is the most important second language in today's world. I think the job of au pair is one which could help me learn better English. I hope very much that you can help me.